AF593756

Fly-Fishing Tactics on Still Water

Also by Geoffrey Bucknall:

BIG PIKE
FISHING DAYS
FLY TYING FOR BEGINNERS
FLY FISHING TACTICS ON RIVERS
RESERVOIR TROUT FISHING

GEOFFREY BUCKNALL

Fly-Fishing Tactics on Still Water

Completely revised

Photographs by
William J. Howes and John Mitchel

Line drawings by
Keith Linsell

FREDERICK MULLER LIMITED
LONDON

First published in Great Britain 1966 by
Frederick Muller Limited
Second revised edition printed 1974
Printed and bound in England by
Redwood Burn Limited
Trowbridge & Esher

CONTENTS

ILLUSTRATIONS

ACKNOWLEDGEMENTS

I WISH to acknowledge the help of the following people in the writing of this book:

John Mitchel and William Howes for taking the excellent pictures in the book; Mr. James Gilmour for advice on the description of the double-haul casting routine; Kenneth Mansfield, for permission to base some sections on articles I had previously written for *Angling*; Mr. William B. Currie for encouraging me to write a 'technical book'; Mr. John Veniard for fly-dressing advice over the years and, of course, to Keith Linsell for his drawings.

G.B.

THE AUTHOR

GEOFFREY BUCKNALL, a dedicated angler from early childhood, is now recognized as one of the leading authorities in this country on fly-tying and it is therefore hardly surprising that his services as a lecturer on this subject are now more widely sought than ever before. The reputation which he has achieved in England through his many books and numerous articles on all aspects of fishing in angling journals, as well as *The Guardian*, has been enhanced by his radio broadcasts both here and abroad, with the result that he is probably as well known on the Continent and in America as he is here.

In the fortunate position of being able to implement his design ideas through his own fishing tackle business, he has also developed an enviable fishery in Sundridge, Kent, in which county he lives with his wife and two sons.

INTRODUCTION

THE FIRST edition of *Fly Fishing Tactics on Still Water*, published in 1966, has proved to be a watershed in the development of this specialised sport. Up to that time the recognized need for distance casting from the bank was achieved by muscular power applied to "heavy" tackle, long slow-actioned rods. Realizing that anglers of moderate physique were being left behind by this common attitude, Geoffrey Bucknall set out to prove that distance could be obtained more easily by using new techniques of casting within a light tackle system.

In the sixties the author was still exploring his new system, and the casting section of the book was also largely exploratory because there was no background experience in Britain for the light, shooting head system. Since then, of course, the whole field of still-water casting has been revolutionised, largely due to the first edition. Ideas which were then experimental have now become acceptable, and this new edition includes the right tackle and technique in definitive form.

That first edition would have justified itself by the new casting routine introduced by Geoffrey Bucknall, yet it went even further, firstly in overturning the opposition to the dry fly, and secondly, in moving still water tactics in the direction of closer imitations of the trout's food, not only in colour, form and size, but also in the way the fauna moves in or on the water.

Also, when the first edition was published, Geoffrey Bucknall was known to the extent of his articles in the angling press and the fly fishing courses he ran in Evening Institutes in London, which were, at the same time, test-beds for his new ideas. Today, he is recognised internationally as a fly-fishing and fly-tying authority, not only for his own books, but also for the contributions he has made to angling literature in France, Scandinavia and North America. Director of firms manufacturing, wholesaling and retailing fishing tackle, he is in the fortunate position of being able to carry through his own design ideas from drawing board to individual angler.

The aspect of his work giving him greatest satisfaction is the creation of the now-famous trout lake at Sundridge, Kent, where huge rainbows are caught every year. Thus he has been deeply involved in the tremendous change in tackle and technique for still water, much of which was introduced for the first time to the British angler by the first edition of *Fly Fishing Tactics on Still Water*.

Instruction, writing and tackle experience would be useless without a fund of fishing experience to support them, and in the actual catching of trout, the author has been constantly in the record books in recent years. The dry-fly catch in Hampshire, five fish totalling over 24 lb; the four Blagdon fish of 12 lb falling to the first morning trial of the Footballer; three trout, each over 6 lb; these are personal landmarks between the two editions.

Above all, though, what strikes the spectator when he sees Geoffrey Bucknall casting is the complete lack of effort and strain. And this, above all, is what he tries to give his readers and pupils—the concept of distance by correct technique with the outright rejection of the old "hit 'em hard and make 'em roll" school. This new revision crystallizes into final and practical form the new casting ideas explored in the first edition; ideas which have virtually changed the whole direction of fly fishing on still water in Britain.

CHAPTER I

TACKLE AND CASTING

THE FIRST edition of *Fly Fishing Tactics on Still Water* brought about such a revolution in technique, not least in distance fly casting, that it is hard to recall the atmosphere before that time. It is interesting to recall the early specialisation of still water fly fishing, and, sadly to say, where it was in error.

The long rod dominated. The simple but fallacious argument was that if you needed to cast further from the bank, then you needed a longer rod. Rods of ten feet were recommended, in heavy split cane. The basic error was that such rods made you tired, and while the first casts of the day unrolled over thirty yards, after an hour or two the muscles began to scream and distance and concentration deteriorated. Fly fishing, which should have been a pleasure, became an endurance test.

Yet another fallacy was the assumption that a long rod cast further merely because of its length. In fact the key to distance casting is line speed in the air, that essential speed needed to drag out a prodigious shoot. It was never clearly understood that the long rod only hurled out a longer line because it required a heavier line to flex the rod. This heavier line moved quickly in the air. Indeed, such long rods were deliberately made with a slow action in order that the line speed would remain within manageable limits. Thus the two factors of line speed and rod action were working against each other, and the resulting strain on the angler of average physique was immense.

The first edition of my book challenged this philosophy, arguing that casting technique within a lighter tackle system would yield distance without fatigue over those very long casting sessions required by the reservoir bank fisherman. There were two difficulties. The first, understandable enough, was the opposition of those brought up in the "old school". The second was the lack of specialised tackle and experience in this country on which to build the new technique.

Theoretically, the first problem should have been overcome by harnessing the experience of tournament casting. Unlike the United States, however, competition casting had diverged from ordinary practical angling and had sought to establish itself as a sport in its own right, virtually divorced from fishing, and with the use of specialised tackle with which no ordinary man could catch fish. There was little dialogue between competition casting and practical fishing, and I discovered that those competitive events once planned with normal gear, the so-called "Skish" contests, were increasingly unpopular among tournament devotees. My attempts to discuss the application of tournament, shooting head methods to still water fly fishing were discouraged.

There was one place where competition casting had actively influenced fly fishing, and this was in the U.S.A. I had bass fishing friends in the Southern States, and later, steelhead and lake trout experts from the East and West of America who unstintingly supplied me with information. This I began to apply to our own trout lakes. It was not easy because it had to be done experimentally, cutting up fly lines to make shooting heads, by trial and error. There was no rod made specifically for shooting head work, and none of the manufacturers I consulted would confess to an interest in breaking the commercial and fishing habit of the long, butt-actioned rod.

That first edition was published while the new casting ideas were yet in their experimental stage. Opposition to it could be guaranteed at "establishment" level. However, the fly-fishing public greedily accepted an option away from those fierce, man-killing rods of the fifties and sixties. The Grafham reservoir opened, a huge expanse of trout-filled water, producing trout of power and dimension never before visualised, and a new generation of men began to compare the contrasting styles offered to them. Writers, previously committed to coarse fishing, began to influence those manufacturers with which they had links, and a new race of fly-rods emerged, made for the shooting head.

This is now history and it was during this time that I had undergone my own development. Having entered, and modestly prospered in the fishing tackle trade myself, I eventually reached the point when I could commission my own tackle designs. The parallel development of the trade had meanwhile switched from split cane fly-rods to those of hollow glass. The solid brass ferrule, which was a dead spot in the old rods, had been replaced by a living joint of the glass spigot. Silk lines, which eventually became incurably sticky, yielded to the plastic flylines, with a choice of different performance to suit its structure, fast, medium and slow sinking lines, floaters and those with sinking tips. Needless to say all of these line-types could be cut for shooting heads.

I was far from satisfied. Some of the old philosophy had spilled over into the new technology and we even had advice to couple heavy shooting heads to the old-fashioned ten foot fly-rod, still a muscle waster, even though the glass feels lighter in the hand. I set to work to make an ideal shooting head rod. What were my terms of reference?

In distance casting, especially when double-hauling, the rod drifts back considerably past the vertical on the back cast, to allow time for the line to extend and space for added leverage on the forward cast. As the rod tip of a nine foot rod is scarcely higher than that of a ten footer at this point, it seems logical to go for the shorter length. Experiments had convinced me that 8 feet 10 inches was the ideal rod length if the correct loading could be compressed into it.

I had already been impressed by the way in which American rod designers vary their tapers within rod lengths which are comfortable to use. For example, an 8½ foot rod, loaded with a size 6 line comprises a "System 6" outfit. If you want to beef up the outfit without increasing rod length, you take a rod taper to suit a size 8 line, the "system 8", in fact. You can tackle up for brook trout right through to steel-head or salmon without being forced to adopt a forest of rods from 7 to 14 feet in individual length.

Having adopted the rod length, I now had to get the action and line loading. Since distance casting must be a question of line speed in the air, I could go for a fastish rod. If such a rod were coupled to a heavy line, then turnover would be fierce enough to cause the fly to crack off. The choice of a normal AFTM 6 line loading was logical, since the rod could then be used ideally for river fly-fishing, or normal dry fly and nymph fishing on still water. By increasing line size, shooting heads of manageable lengths could be cut from double-taper fly-lines. Thus 33 feet of an ATFM 8, or 36 feet of AFTM 7, ideally load the "Two Lakes" fly-rod, as my ideal was named, after the famous fly-fishery where I put the prototype through its paces.

Those readers who have patiently followed this technical discussion will have realised that I had introduced a light-shooting head system for still water fly-fishing to give good working distance for the bank fisherman, and to go on giving it hour after hour without fatigue. As the debate developed, I also realised that this wasn't enough.

Many anglers accepted the new casting system. Others preferred to continue with the normal, full length fly-line because there are certain unpleasant handling characteristics of the nylon shooting line spliced to shooting heads. There is some justice in this, so the next stage was to devise a tackle system to yield good distance with normal fly-lines, while convincing anglers that, even for this traditional approach, they didn't need the old, longbow rod. This involved both a new rod and a new line.

The rod would need to be powerful within a nine foot length of glass. The line would need to be as close as possible to the shooting head profile, but in a single, plastic coated unit. I was asking for a nine-foot system 8 rod with medium-fast action. The line would have a fine tip, to give perfect turnover of the leader at distance, plus a fine shooting line behind a shortish steeply tapered belly. It struck me that the arguments for long belly lines were incorrect, since the longer the casting-weight part of a line, the more easily it loses its impetus in the air.

So my "Powercast" rod was added to the "Two Lakes", the former for distance casting with the new "Fast Taper" fly-line, the latter for use with shooting heads, or casting a normal, light line on lake or river. The new rod soon revealed itself as a firm favourite and comparative novices were realising the extremely difficult act of throwing an entire 30 yard fly-line beyond the rod tip, as was witnessed many times at the Sundridge Trout Lake where it was put on test for any interested caster. I was delighted when the undoubted "guttiness" behind campaigning for new methods eventually triumphed, bringing with it a new family of fly-tackle for distance casting, achieved for the first time without that fatigue factor built into the old school of rods.

The first edition of this book could hardly be directed at beginners, much though I expected it to teach them. The jargon cannot be omitted in expressing a new idea-system in any sport. Let me now get down to some basics. What, essentially is a shooting head? How do you make it?

The shooting head is only the working part of a fly-line, cut from its parent double-taper, and joined to a finer, shooting line of nylon monofilament. It is obvious that the head must be a ratio of weight to length, the weight sufficient to flex the rod, the length manageable in the air. Experience shows that between 30 and 36 feet of line, one or two sizes up on that normally recommended for the rod, is the best formula. Some writers have taken the easy option, that the exact length/weight of the head isn't critical. They are wrong. A shooting head bought over the counter blindly is a risk.

You should buy half a fly-line, size as described above, and run it onto your fly-reel. Cast it into different directions of wind until you have a comfortable length in the air which flexes the rod. The acid test is this: does it want to pull back on the back-cast? You cannot double haul unless it does so. Measure the line at this stage, from tip to rod top, and if it falls within the limits I've mentioned, cut it at the rod-tip. That length of double-taper line, so cut, is your shooting head. It can be from any type of line you wish, floating to fast-sinking.

Given a balance, you can use this head as a master against which to weigh out other heads, the materials of which have different gravities, hence varying belly diameters. Put your master shooting head in one balance pan, then an overweight head in the other. You clip back from the butt of the new head until the two weights equalise. It is a fast and efficient method. I whip in small loops to the butts and tips of my heads by softening the plastic coat in cellulose varnish thinners over an inch of line, scrape it away from the braided core, which is then whipped back on itself with a fine thread, finally varnished.

Thus shooting heads of various types can be carried, loosely coiled in plastic bags, and interchanged on the reel drum as required. Of course, the loop and knot will "tick" against the tip ring of the rod, but once the nylon shooting line is stretched and working well, it is time-wasting to start fishing afresh with another reel or drum and unstretched shooting line. For me, the shooting head is for fishing at long range. I rarely fish the fly out to my feet, but I roll the line off the water as soon as the join hits the tip ring, going straight into the next cast.

Distance fly casting is double-hauling, which on the back-cast, straightens the line, keeps it high and fast, and, on the following forward cast, speeds the line to pull out a prodigious line-shoot. Now, what is double-hauling? The average, competent fly-caster performs two arm and rod movements. The first is called the "back cast" in which the forearm lifts the rod smartly, roughly level with the ear. Wrist and thumb pressure stop the rod at this point so that the rod flexes backwards against the anchoring wrist, and the line streams out behind. The "forward-cast" is the opposite movement, when the forearm drives the rod forwards and downwards so that the line streams out over the water. Normally, the left hand pulls line downwards from the rod ring on the back cast, releasing it as a "shoot" on the termination of the forward-cast. This is the "single haul".

The double haul is when two left-hand pulls of line are fitted in to the casting sequence, with a feed back of line between them. Roughly speaking, the first haul coincides with the back-cast, the feed back with the pause between the two rod movements, and the second haul with the forward-cast. The exact sequence is shown in the illustrated appendix.

The casting routine should be studied separately, either from the instructions shown, or else with the help of a competent instructor. Some things need to be driven home at the outset.

In my experience, most common errors happen at the wrist, and it is at the wrist that they can be checked and cured. We know the weak wrist of the beginner is his commonest fault. I'm not concerned with that here. The experienced caster may not appreciate that his wrist, too, can be at fault when he reaches out for distance. Instead of the beginner's fault of the wrist hinging backwards at the summit of the back-cast, his wrist is likely to twist outwards as the rod is thrown back. The line crosses itself, the hook fouls the leader, falling into a huge loop in front of the caster. If he were to watch his wrist he would see the reel drum turning outwards on the back-cast when it should stay parallel to the ground.

When I've been teaching double haul, the "pupils" always try to haul the line too vigorously. It's amazing how little the line needs to be pulled to speed the shoot. The two hauls must be sweet, even gentle, and flowing together. Jerky, ferocious hauls of line achieve little, other than to ruin the timing of the cast.

The great advantage of my shorter and lighter shooting heads was that they scaled down a competition distance method to one attainable by every practical angler. He should be aiming at a reasonable working distance, not the ultimate erroneous estimates made by optimistic journalists. They sometimes glibly claim a forty yard cast made to intercept a fish. Forty yeards is one hell of a way, and until you've made thirty yards, measured it, you cannot realise the task of getting another ten when up to your bottom in the margins of a lake, plus contrary winds, rising bank behind, and so forth. I think forty yards casts are very rare indeed in normal fishing! Aim at a minimum of thirty, with a good turnover of leader and fly. Keep this up for long periods with the minimum of casting routines, and that's good fishing. Averages mean silky timing, ultimates mean tiring arm jerks.

For the truth is that the fallacious thinking behind the old "long rod" was that muscle became the substitute for technique, the "hit 'em a bloody sight harder" error of hoary casting instructors. If tournament men had ever tried to influence still water fly-casting, they would have had to adapt to the sheer length of time we fish through, even from dawn to dusk.

Double haul casting is easiest with the shooting head. The purpose of the finer, shooting nylon is to reduce line friction through the rod rings. As a result, feeding back line between the two hauls is fairly easy. With the normal fly-line, many casters have trouble in the feed-back. The reason is that they fail to put enough steam into the back cast, a common fault in both beginner and experienced caster alike. The beginner tends to throw his back-cast weakly, then thrash forward with muscle power. Viewing the fly-rod as a spring, it must be wound up firmly before it can release energy on the forward-cast. The good-enough caster, though, doesn't realise that it "feels wrong" to make a powerful back-cast. Yet even if the back-cast feels stronger than the forward one, the muscles deceive. It is hard indeed to make the back-cast either as fast as the forward-cast, or as fast as it ought to be, simply because it is an unaccustomed muscle movement. Push the rod back with decision, you can feed back a normal fly-line.

And what else? The common cry against conversion! There just isn't enough time to fit two line hauls into the space of a fly-casting routine. I know it feels that way—at first. I've described the ordinary, single line haul of the average fly-caster. The way to convert to double haul is to fit this single pull and release into the forward-cast alone. You simply keep the line taut on the back-cast, left hand going back with the rod, then pulling down sweetly on the forward-cast, shooting in the normal way. Of the two hauls, the second one does three-quarters of the work, the first being mainly to straighten line, and to get the line moving through the rings, thus overcoming inertia. When the haul is fitted comfortably into the forward cast, it is then a natural development to place the first haul in its proper place.

Reels have developed considerably since 1966. Today we have lightweight geared models which allow a fast rate of line retrieve. Although I still prefer to control a fast running fish by handling the line, when it does give up the struggle, it's sensible to wind the loose line onto the drum, if only to stop falling over it. I rule out automatic fly-reels for distance casting. Their considerable weight alone is against them, and I've yet to meet one with sufficient line capacity. I've seen two good Test trout lost because the fly was zipped out of the jaw just as the fish flurried on the surface. For me, in playing a fish, instinctive feeling to give, hold or recover line must not give way to mechanical gadgetry, however sophisticated. Geared reels, though, are a boon.

In fishing books, it's customary to list heaps of useful accessories, but bags and nets are matters of choice and common sense. There are still one or two major items where performance and safety are involved.

Waders are vital. They must be comfortable and safe. The old, heavy hob-nailed boot never seemed tremendously safe to me, especially when the studs were shiny and worn. The wader of my choice is called "Griplastic", made by the French firm of Hutchinson. The non-slip soles are the product of modern research, cleated in such a way as to resist slip in any direction. Moreover they clip down for walking, have belt attachments at front and back to stop the old trouble of sagging, and they tend to cling tightly, so that I don't slop about in them.

Fly-hooks are vital, for it their temper is faulty, all we attempt goes for naught. In the early seventies, coarse fishermen were using a new French hook, called simply the "Specimen" hook. It successfully beat huge carp at Redmire Lake, up to 43 lb though still being fine in wire. Unfortunately it was straight eyed and short of shank. In 1972 I visited the manufacturer, Viellard-Migeon, in France, where I was given the run of the machine shops, with technical help, to develop this hook into a wide gape fly-hook, which the maker graciously decided to market in my own name, as the "Geoffrey Bucknall" fly-hook. This is one aspect of our trade, whereby most members of it are keen anglers and where they can, they try to interpret their own ideas into products, so that enthusiasm transcends normal marketing. Anyone can make and sell fly-hooks. Enthusiasts improve the breed beyond commercial needs.

Thus we will now have the fly-tying version of a hook which swept coarse fishing, longer in shank, with shorter barb and point, down eye and up eye, and with the renowned French temper. It is rare for the angler to intervene in hook design, keen though he may be to develop his rods and reels. Strange this is, the hook being the actual war-head of our fly-casting missile.

In the early days, line rafts and trays were no part of our equipment, so preoccupied were we with developing the practical application of the light shooting-head system. Line trays tend to bunch the shooting line rather tightly, leading to occasional tangles when the shoot tries to pull it upwards. You can drop wider loops onto a floating raft, which need be no more than a small cycle inner tube inflated inside a plastic bag, and attached to the wader with cord and suction pad.

Leaders, too, are important and the practical man makes

his own. What are the requirements? Firstly, that the step-down in diameter between fly-line point and leader butt should be no more than one third. The "Fast Taper" fly-lines are deliberately designed with fine points to assist turnover, but some plastic fly-lines have tips of too great a diameter, necessitating the whipping of a collar of thicker nylon between the line and the leader.

The nylon, being close to the fish, must be free from glitter. This is best arranged by rubbing polished nylons down to a dull grey with a fine abrasive powder. I found "Vim" to be first class for this.

Leaders should be soft and free from coil and cling so that they straighten and cut through the surface film, right from the first cast of the day. This is achieved by placing the leaders between leaves of felt, damped with a 10% glycerine solution. Overnight treatment is quite sufficient to make the nylon supple.

In general terms, we need a short, steeply tapered leader of about seven feet for pushing into strong winds. Our normal leaders will be balanced at nine feet, while an ultra-long leader for calm, bright conditions, could be up to twelve feet in length. We mistakenly equate nylon diameter with breaking strains when choosing nylon, but as this error is widespread I must concede to it by advising that blood-knots should only be used to link nylons differing by no more than 2 lb b.s. Wider differences should be joined by doubling the finer nylon of the blood-knot to balance the opposite side of the knot, the so-called Stu Apte knot.

The common sense rule is to avoid tying too small a fly to a thick leader point which cannot let it hinge freely. A large fly on a weak nylon point will hinge too freely and soon break away.

Two other factors must be mentioned in discussing casting and tackle. The first is the high gloss finish applied to many fly-rods. Since glass absorbs only a minute amount of moisture, the only purpose of glass varnish is to display the rod for sale. In action, the rod flashes. I have frequently seen surface feeding fish bolt in panic from the light reflected from such a rod. The standard finish of my rods is a dull matt. I consider it sheer folly to reduce one's chances by using a highly varnished rod—fly-fishing is tough enough already.

I am equally certain that the argument in favour of the white fly-line is erratic. Alas, white lines are invariably polished, too, and I have seen them scare fish, so avoid bright colours and brilliant finish in any floating line. I go for the pale green or drab olive, myself. The trout is a wary creature and you cannot err too far on the side of caution.

I've been talking about the general tackle and casting methods for bank fishing. There are occasions when we need specialised gear. Boat fishing is one of these. I know some anglers use boats as floating casting platforms, standing up to saw out a long line. It is dangerous. On large waters, it is frequently better to fish a long drift, seated comfortably. The rod should be long so that the dropper-flies can be worked attractively. As fish take close to the boat on a tight line, the rod must be limber enough to absorb the sudden shock of a violent lunge at the fly. The "Powercast", for example, might be too powerful to avoid the rupture of a fine nylon point at such close range.

I developed for this fishing a light ten footer, the line loading of which was only for an AFTM 5, or 6 at most. The rod doubles up perfectly for downstream wet fly-fishing, as well as dapping.

Another option is for dry fly-fishing, not only because it is successful when conditions indicate, but it can be one of the most interesting tactics to employ. The problem of intercepting rising fish is that of being able to switch suddenly both direction and distance, as one rise proves fruitless while another materialises in another place. The "Two Lakes" rod is ideal for this, but it is better to change to a double-taper floating line which can be rolled off the water to avoid drowning the fly when it needs to be lifted and recast from long range. The shooting head suits wake-fly fishing, when a large dry fly is deliberately retrieved on the surface to imitate a moth trapped in the surface film. In true dry fly-work, the floater is put to the rising fish. During either a hatch of duns or sedge, fish will be seen taking floating natural fly in large numbers and the fishing method requires continual interceptions with the matching artificial fly.

On still water we rarely require the range of specialised casts employed by the all-round river expert. Steeple casts are not needed to throw a short, high line above an obstacle behind. Roll casts are only for unsticking the line prior to making the next cast. Side casting, ambidextrous work, and distance roll casting are unnecessary, but the bank angler does need to master strong winds into his teeth or across his body.

The so-called "storm cast" into the wind consists of a low, late punch on the forward cast, making a high back-cast. The trick is to allow a longer pause than usual, drop the wrist and hammer the line through, as if you were aiming "under the wind". As in all of these descriptions, assuming you are right handed, if the wind blows into your right ear, it also takes the fly behind your neck on the back-cast. You must lay the rod over to the right and throw the line away from your body on the back-cast, giving it room to come through safely on the forward punch.

Let me sum up the conclusions of this chapter.

Firstly it is clear that most of us are tempted to use rods beyond our physique but that increased distance can be obtained without fatigue by using a lighter outfit with correct double-haul technique. Now that hollow glass holds sway in rod manufacture, don't make the mistake of thinking that the weight of a rod is the fatigue factor. The important thing is the muscle power needed to flex the rod, regardless of its weight. We can now make man-killing rods as light as a feather.

Secondly, I argue that the light shooting head system will give you good working distances without fatigue and without loss of finesse in presentation, with the proviso that the balance of the rod, head and leader is good. I concede that shooting heads are uncomfortable, but that the lighter, fast rod will give you greater distance over long periods even with normal fly-line than some of the longer, slower rods labelled "Reservoir".

Lastly, the evil to avoid is the combination of the worst of both styles, a long slow rod loaded with a heavy shooting head. Shooting heads made from lines of AFTM 9 and upwards would normally travel at such speed in the air as to ruin finesse. Therefore some advocate the absurdity of a rod to slow down the air-speed of the head, which really is a tiring business.

Do this for me. When you have mastered distance with the light outfit, switch to the longer rod, and see if you can outcast yourself. It's the story of the tree-trunk bat in the hands of the village blacksmith. He clumsily heaves sixes into the churchyard. The little chap, he works on his timing, stroking away four after four, using the speed of the ball. He builds up a ton over two hours or so, while the blacksmith, pint in hand, is brooding on why he just can't put together a useful innings of spectacular soaring boundaries.

Don't base your tackle on the powerful man, admire him though you might. Work on the technique. You may well be outcasting him an hour later, with no strain. That's what it's all about.

CHAPTER II

FLY DRESSING FOR STILL WATER

UNDER NORMAL circumstances there are even strong reasons why fly-fishermen should dress their own artificials. It is not merely a question of economy. In spite of the arguments summed up as "choice of fly versus presentation", the two are inseparable. The angler must be concerned about the behaviour of his fly in the water, for although it is scarcely possible to analyse what it is about the fly, its silhouette or colour, that triggers off the feeding reflex in the fish, movement in the water plays a vital part. This fly behaviour is born at the fly-dressing vice, for even the simplest pattern can be designed to float or sink, ride high or low in the water. In other words, the fisherman dresses flies to serve his own particular tactics. Sometimes this is by tailoring traditional flies to personal taste, such as by making wet-flies with low, slim wings in the manner advocated by "Lemon Grey" for his fishery on the River Torridge. Or another angler might start from scratch and produce a new and revolutionary series of flies to suit his own theories, as was the case with the "Ivens" series of lake flies.

At the time of writing, something in the nature of a minor crisis is approaching the fly-dressing industry. This is due to a combination of two circumstances. The "trade" is finding it increasingly difficult to compete with light industry to attract labour. Young girls prefer to work in modern factories where they can earn higher wages in pleasant surroundings. The second factor is the shortage of certain materials, notably good-quality hackles.

The result is an inevitable increase in the price of flies, together with a shortage of many of the unusual patterns. For this reason, I am including a chapter on fly-tying in this book, and this will enable me to marry each fly-fishing tactic to the appropriate fly-dressing. Normally it would need a full book to do justice to the subject of fly-dressing, but fortunately a good number of the flies we need in reservoir fishing are of simple structure.

I will begin with a survey of the tools and materials needed for the preparation of these patterns.

The first essential is an efficient vice. These may be bought from suppliers like Veniard, but the handyman should be able to turn out a presentable one. I saw a suitable vice made from a pair of long-nosed pliers, the handles of which had been drilled to take a long bolt and butterfly nut. One of these handles had been extended to form a clamp for the bench. I recommend that you should otherwise procure the best vice that you can afford, for the cheaper models can be frustrating to work with if the hooks slip about between the jaws.

Hackle pliers must also be obtained. It is wise to have two pairs, one of medium weight for normal hackles, and a light-weight pair for smaller feathers. A pair of surgical scissors is also required. A dubbing needle is easily made by pushing a large darning needle into a cork. Such instruments as winging pliers, bobbin-holders and whip-finishing tools are not strictly necessary, for the fingers will do their functions more effectively.

The tying thread normally used in fly-tying is made from silk, but many modern dressers are coming to prefer nylon thread. I employ the nylon that girls use to repair their stockings. It cost a copper or two for a card of 50 yards and it comes in various shades of black and brown. This thread is finer, yet stronger than silk. Furthermore it is rotproof, unlike silk. There are one or two fly patterns whose bodies are formed from a tying silk. One such fly is the Greenwell, while another is the Partridge and Orange. Silks in these colours will be preferable to substitutes.

There can be no substitute for hackles, though a few of our

lake patterns, notably some invented by Ivens, do not have any. Failing the offices of a friendly farmer or poultryman, they must be purchased from a dealer. It is more economical to buy these feathers on the neck rather than in elegant cellophane packets containing a dozen or so graded by size. Even so, firms such as Veniard will sell bargain packs of whole necks by the dozen and half-dozen at very reasonable prices, providing that you are willing to take a chance with the colours. Hackles are the feathers from the necks of game and domestic poultry, usually the latter. The hackles from a cockerel of three or more years of age are quite stiff and sheeny, therefore being used for the legs of dry-flies. Hen hackles are soft and downy, and are normally used in wet-flies.

A cape is the word used to describe a whole neck of feathers, and not only does it hold hackles of various sizes, but there are often subtle changes of colour in the same neck. Necks of both cockerel and hen should be gathered in the principal colours, black, white, red, ginger. Other shades, such as olive and blue, must be dyed, but the dyes are bought cheaply from the dealers and the procedure is simple and far from messy. Bi-coloured hackles are now becoming very hard to procure, particularly for dry-flies. If the opportunity arises, Red and Black (Furnace) and Badger (Black and White) should be snapped up. In each case, the darker colour forms the centre of the feather, that is to say, the "list".

Besides hackles, wing and tail feathers from certain birds must be obtained to make the wings of the fly. A friendly gun may supply you with invaluable plumage from pheasant, partridge, mallard, woodcock, or grouse. If you have a strong stomach, never neglect the corpses of starlings and blackbirds that fall victim to the car or air-gun, while the long-suffering domestic fowl will provide even more. The colours of importance are red, white and grey. Fly-dressers learn to walk with their eyes on the ground on their country strolls.

Body materials are an easier proposition. The needlework basket can be raided for wools, and even modern fluorescent ones may spring to light. While browsing in the local haberdashery, I came upon some reels of gold and silver lurex at a couple of shillings for 75 yards, and this deals with all my needs in making "flashers". Some herls will still have to be bought, and peacock is essential, as well as some packets of seal's fur dyed in different shades, especially claret.

Finally, there are hairs and furs. The former are now becoming popular for the making of tube-flies, hair-wings and streamer flies, but initially, a grey and brown squirrel tail will suffice. In the second category, the fur from certain pelts forms the body for a host of well-known patterns. Rabbit, water-rat, and mole should all be easy to find, but a pair of hare's ears are a different proposition. You ask one of the greyhounds at the local dog-track! Even so, these materials can all be bought cheaply from the dealer.

Of course, there are things that I have left out. Some of them will be introduced in later chapters, but this makes a solid foundation. The best plan is to start from small beginnings, building up the collection around a handful of favourite flies, then expanding it to take in further patterns. The materials should be stored in cigar boxes or drawers, and sprinkled with naphtha to counteract the ravages of moth and feather-mite. Never forget the value of experimentation. I have a friend who swears by a nymph, the body of which he makes from the cotton wool of an Aspirin bottle.

Having dealt with the "why" of fly-dressing, I must now tell you how to set about making your first pattern. But firstly I must point out that these earliest efforts will catch fish. Try them! The fly I have chosen is the "Black and Peacock Spider" from the stable of the inventive Mr. Ivens. I was introduced to this fly on reading his classic book, already mentioned, and I have made some wonderful bags with it. I must emphasise, though, that I am discussing fly-dressing procedures generally in describing how to fashion this fly.

There are only two basic operations in fly-dressing. If it is realised that an artificial fly is made by fixing various materials to a hook shank with a thread, then it is immediately obvious that this can only be done in two ways:

1. By tying a material at an angle to the hook shank, and winding this material round the hook shank.

2. By binding a material to the shank of the hook so as to be parallel to it.

All fly-dressing operations are based on these two principles.

Only the first of these two principles is involved in the preparation of the fly that I have chosen, this simple wet-fly pattern. This fly consists of one body material, peacock herl, and a hackle, black hen. Here are the procedures.

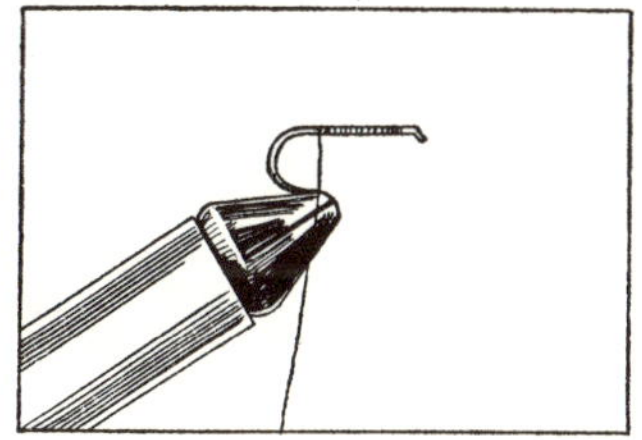

Fig. 1

A piece of white paper or board is placed on the bench to reflect the light from a nearby table lamp whose rays are directed to the area. The vice is clamped down to the bench, using the white paper as a background. The tools, hackle-pliers, scissors, dubbing needle and a razor blade are laid out to hand, together with the materials I have mentioned.

A size 10 hook is selected and firmly fixed in the vice so that the jaws grip the "bite" of the hook and mask its point. Down-turned eyes are preferred for the hooks of wet-flies, in order that the eye will act as a miniature diving vane when the fly is drawn through the water. Now, before anything else, the hook must be given a strong tweak to test its temper; if it breaks in a hefty trout, it would be the angler whose temper would be tested.

Next, the tying thread is wound on to the hook shank (Fig. 1) so that it covers two-thirds of the shank from a point near the eye to the beginning of the bend. This stage, though simple, is most important, for it determines the length of the body. Sufficient room must be left between the end of the body and the eye of the hook to allow the hackle to be wound in and the fly finished off with a varnished head. The point of insertion of the thread can thus mark the place beyond which the body material must not be wound.

Three or four strands of bronze-coloured peacock herl with a good flue are tied in at the hook bend in such a way as the thread pinches the herls against the underside of the hook. The thread is wound back over the stubs of the herl, which

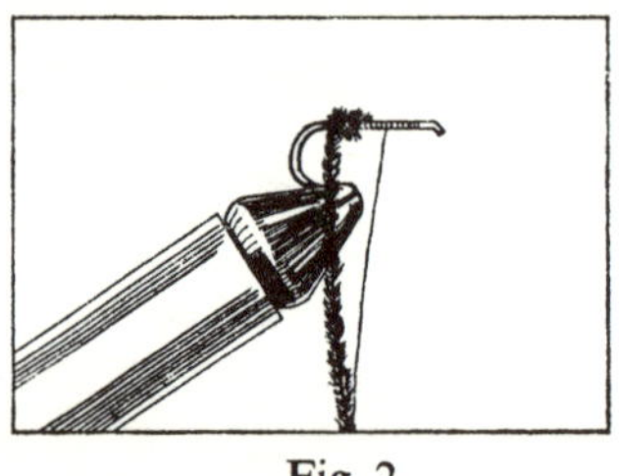

Fig. 2

Fig. 3

need not be trimmed flush to the shank as they lend substance to the body. The thread is thus taken back to its point of origin, and it is a good exercise to ensure that all turns of the thread are evenly wound (Fig. 2). The herls are now twirled together, and then also wound along the hookshank in a clockwise direction to make a fuzzy body up to the tying thread, which is nipped in the hackle pliers or tension button to keep it taut (Fig. 3). Herls are not invariably twisted round each other, but only when a chubby effect is desired. It is not a desirable practice with finer herls, such as heron or pheasant tail. The herls are finally bound down, and the spare ends clipped off.

With the body now occupying two-thirds of the shank, the hackle is prepared by stripping away the fluffy fibres from the bottom of the feather, leaving a central stalk. This is tied into the fly immediately in front of the body with a figure-of-eight tying, so that the hackle is at right angles to the hook (Fig. 4). It is important that the duller side of the hackle should face to the rear of the hook, that is to say the hackle bulges towards the eye. Holding the thread to the rear of the hackle, the pliers are nipped on to the tip of the feather, which is then given two turns round the shank in a direction away from

Fig. 4

the dresser, and then left to hang by weight of the pliers. The thread is then carefully wound back through the hackle, thus binding it down securely. The unused remainder of the feather may then be trimmed away, flush with the fly. It only remains to build up a small head to the fly with a few turns of thread, whip-finish and varnish; then the fly is ready for action.

Although two or three half-hitches will serve to secure the head of the fly, it is worth while mastering the whip-finish, for it is essential in the preparation of winged flies. A whip-finish is simply a loop binding down its free end, which is then pulled tight through the turns and cut away.

I will pause before describing the second principle of fly-dressing. I know that it takes some time before the fingers become accustomed to working in miniature. It feels as if you have five sausages on your hands that just refuse to execute the dictates of your brain or follow the guidance of your eye. I can assure you this stage will pass, and your fingers will develop that certain "feel" that watchmakers and surgeons know so well. As I instruct a class of some two dozen anglers in fly-dressing, I have first-hand opportunity to observe the growth of this strange adaption. Men who work in a variety of trades, those who operate huge machines by day, manipulate feather and fur in the evenings. I watch the flies change, week by week, from an unrecognisable concoction to a perfect fly I should be proud to claim as my own.

With the mastery of these elementary stages so far discussed, dozens of effective patterns are within your grasp, killing patterns like the Grouse and Orange, or Ivens' other nymphs.

For example, if the wet-fly's hen hackle were to be substituted for a cock's hackle and given an extra turn or two, the ordinary dry-fly has been made. If a brown and white hackle were added, one after the other, to the peacock-herl body, the result would be a dry Coachman! Already the permutations are endless.

Now is the time to practise each stage until it is mastered. If you can also receive skilled tuition, it will save much trial and error. At the moment, there are few courses in fly-dressing, and most of these exist in game-fishing areas, the Forces or in one or two hospitals for occupational therapy. I believe my own courses are the only ones devoted entirely to the subject in the London area, but I am sure that the changing situation in the fly-tying trade is going to create an increased demand that will have to be met.

To return to our spider-type wet-fly, how can this pattern be taken a stage further to convert it into an orthodox winged fly? The addition of wings to a fly demonstrates the second principle of dressing, that of tying materials parallel to the hook.

Going back to the stage when the hackle has been secured,

the hackle fibres are divided on top of the hook into two equal sections, and then pulled down below the shank. This is easily accomplished if the fingers are first moistened. The hackle is kept in this position with two or three diagonal turns of thread (Fig. 5). Before preparing the wing slips, a bed must be made

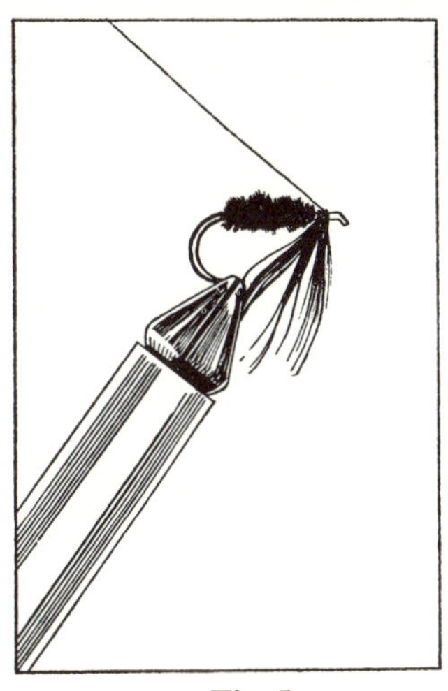

Fig. 5

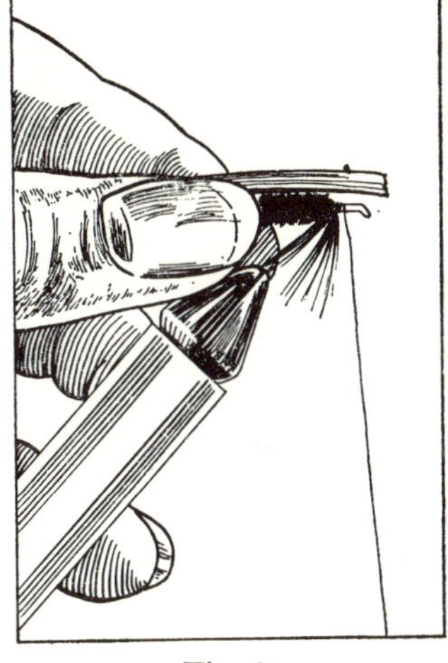

Fig. 6

for them in front of the hackle with a few turns of the thread, for wings must never be tied down to a bare hook shank. This is also a stage that will help to determine the style of dressing, for the higher this bed is built up in relation to the bunch of hackle fibres behind it, the lower will the wings lie along the hook.

The wings are prepared by cutting two matching slips of feather from opposing wing-feathers. These slips will have the same natural curve as their parent feathers. By positioning these slips so that they curve inwards towards each other, the wet-fly wings are prepared, while slips curving outwards are used for dry-flies. In winging, it is vital to ensure that they are on straight and do not twist. Therefore the tying thread must pull the fibres down on top of each other, and on to the centre of the hook shank. This is done by holding the slips in the required position with the left hand, while making a loose loop of thread over them (Fig. 6). This loop is also gripped between the fingers and thumb of the left hand, with the wing slips through it. The thread is then pulled tight, and tension applied to keep the wings in position (Fig. 7). If the

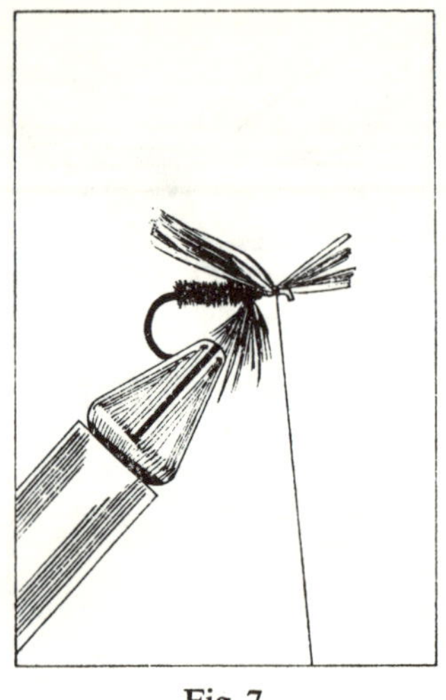

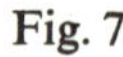

Fig. 7

Fig. 8

wings appear to be satisfactory, a whip finish is applied, the roots cut away flush with the shank, and the fly finished off (Fig. 8).

Winging is not easy, and there is a temptation to use a special tool. I counsel lots of practice with the fingers, and then that certain "feel" will develop. It is better to start with strong feathers like duck or woodcock, rather than the teal and mallard breast feathers which tend to split and twist more readily.

If the wings are put on so that the matching slips curve outwards, the upright-winged dry-fly can be prepared. Before the roots are trimmed away, the wings are raised in the upright position, and a few turns of tying silk behind the wings, as well as one turn round their base, will hold them in position. The hackle is wound in last on a dry-fly, and I find it a good plan to make the first two turns in front of the wings, and then make three good turns behind them to add reinforcement.

It must be confessed that, although the traditional winged dry-fly is beautiful to behold, it is on the way out. Anglers realise that these wings are obscured to the trout by the dressing of the fly. Perhaps they do add a certain poise to the fly, and artists love to feature the fly drifting down the current of a chalk-stream to the waiting fish, its wings cocked cheekily like the sails of a tiny yacht. But they serve no practical purpose other than to show off the fly-dresser's art.

I must briefly mention some other processes that lake anglers will need to know.

Many flies require a tail, usually made from a few fibres of a large hackle identical to that wound in at the throat. They are tied in a bunch on top of the hook before the body material is attached. Instead of twitching away the stubs of these fibres, it is a good plan to bind them down to the hook shank when winding the thread back towards the eye of the hook. Dry-flies can have their tails cocked up in realistic way by putting an additional turn of the thread round the hook shank, but under the tail fibres after they have been tied in.

Some flies are dressed with bodies of fur or wool. Instead of tying in a piece of this material, it is teased out and spun round the thread, which has previously been waxed to make it stick (Fig. 9). The thread, now coated with the fur or wool, is wound up the shank to form the body. With a body dubbed in this way, it is usual to have a wire or tinsel ribbed diagonally over it for protection against the sharp teeth of the trout. This wire is tied in at the hook-bend before the body is formed, then spiralled up the body before the hackle and wings are put on. I prefer to wind my ribbing in the opposite direction to the body-material to stop it being buried between the turns of the dressing.

It is easier to spin a dubbing to a thread that is held taut, but coarse furs, such as seal, should be mixed with a similarly coloured wool. Good effects can be achieved by blending in materials of different shades, or those which are fluorescent.

A number of flies, including the sedges, have a hackle wound down the body diagonally, from the neck to the tail. Such a hackle is said to be "palmered", an expression thought to date to the times of the Crusades when knights returning from the Holy Land carried branches of palm trees. A wire

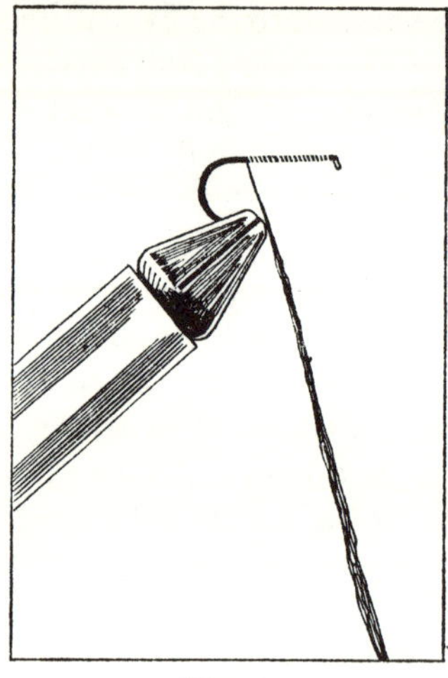

Fig. 9

or tinsel ribbing is tied in at the bend of the hook before the body is made, and this is wound up over the hackle in the opposite direction, to make it secure (Figs. 10, 11).

These sedge-flies, together with moths, can be winged conveniently with an inch or so of feather rolled up like a carpet. This roll is simply tied on in the usual way, and it divides itself automatically to make a deadly copy of the natural flies.

This concludes a thumbnail description of the fly-dressing styles used for most lake flies. It has, of necessity, been a basic outline of a fascinating art that would need an entire book to cover. My intention is twofold. I want to whet your appetite sufficiently to encourage you to take the plunge and learn to fashion your own artificials. I also wish to show you the structure of these flies, and how technique at the work-bench determines the behaviour of the lure in the water.

If you now wish to take this subject further, I advise you to

Fig. 10 Fig. 11

buy or borrow a competent handbook on it, such as John Veniard's "Fly-Dresser's Guide".

Having introduced the mechanics of fly-dressing, I wish to comment on the underlying philosophy of fly-choice on still water. I reiterate that change was slow to come to the artificial fly used on lake and loch. The fisherman was quite content with slightly larger versions of river flies, which are based on the plumage of a game bird, with a range of furs or wools in various hues for the bodies. Thus a Woodcock and Green could become a Grouse and Green or a Teal and Green acording to personal taste. The theory that prevailed was to use a bright fly on a dull day, and vice versa.

Yet anglers with inventive minds have turned to reservoir

fishing in recent years, and change came suddenly. Traditions were shaken by the book on still-water fly-fishing written by T. C. Ivens, which introduced a revolutionary series of flies constructed strictly according to their mechanical behaviour in the water. Lightly dressed patterns were devised to swim high in the water, heavier ones at greater depth. Even so, these artificials still conformed to the basic definitions of dull "deceivers" and bright "attractors".

Many traditionalists frowned at the innovation of lake flies without wings, for many of them were nothing more than dyed ostrich herls twirled around the hook. But the simple shapes did pay tribute to the cult of distance casting, by reducing air resistance, while these nymphs cut through the surface film without any bother. Above all, most of his artificials can be fashioned by the most spatulate-fingered angler.

It is strange that reservoir fishermen had never produced a "Halford" with his insistence on exact imitation. Never, that is, until C. F. Walker wrote his book *Lake Flies and their Imitation*. The most important insect on the chalk-stream is the "dayfly", as I like to term it, which belongs to the order Ephemeridae. These "dayflies" also exist in still water, as exemplified by the Lake Olive, and although they do not have the same food value to the trout as sedges and midges, it was only a question of time before someone recognised their importance.

Walker did far more than create a number of copies for the Dayfly Duns and Spinners. He simulated a whole range of lake dwellers, from the busy Water-Boatman to the gaudy Damsel Fly. As a fly-dresser, he posed me a nice problem, for I had to add a fresh range of materials to my cabinet and learn some new techniques of dressing.

Since these two schools of thought have so recently emerged, no rationalisation of them has taken place. The newcomer to lake fly-fishing is faced with a medley of three systems. There is the hotchpotch of traditional teal or mallard winged patterns, together with the utilitarian Ivens Flies and dozens of copies of lake insects invented by Walker. One of the objects of this book is to chart a passage through these reefs.

And now I must declare my interest. I hold it to be true that lake trout feed mainly on insects and fly. At times, this feeding becomes preoccupied, which is to say that the fish feeds exclusively on a single food-form, usually when this is in profusion in an area. I do not believe that a trout harrying a shoal of minnows will turn aside to snap at a sedge-fly. There are other times when trout seem to be aimlessly cruising along, taking an odd morsel of food here and there.

Preoccupied feeding usually reveals itself by surface disturbance and the appearance of the food supply. The secret lies in recognising the food and copying it both in size, shape and colour from the fly box, but also in behaviour. And for the moody feeder, I shall also suggest some tactics.

CHAPTER III

BOAT FISHING

IT IS possible to hire a boat on nearly all of our trout reservoirs. Even though it costs more to fish from a boat than the bank, the cost can be shared by a partner. The conditions of the boats vary from place to place, but I find most of them reasonably well maintained, and particularly so at Weir Wood reservoir, in Sussex, and the Bristol lakes. On some waters it is also possible to employ a ghillie for the day, though it goes without saying that the cost is even higher. At the luxury end of the scale, on Chew lake you may take out a boat fitted with an outboard motor, but this is the most expensive way of fishing a reservoir. On some waters you may start boat fishing as soon as the bank anglers begin operations, while on others you may not row out until 10 a.m.

I have already mentioned the question of cushions and drogues, but I would also caution you against taking it for granted that each boat will be supplied with a huge net. They are provided on Chew and Blagdon. On other waters they are absent.

So far for the hard facts. But what about that eternal controversy that raises its hoary head wherever fly-fishermen congregate? Which is best, boat or bank. Statistically speaking, I imagine that the boat anglers catch more fish, but the strange thing is that I often notice that the bank anglers have killed the heaviest specimens. Why is this?

In a lake like Chew, I believe that the really great trout feed heavily on fry in the early morning, before the boats are allowed out, and they subsequently retire to deep water. I have seen some of these monsters making forays into the shallows at first light, and they are easily recognisable by the tremendous disturbance of the surface. They seem to sweep into the shallow bays for just an hour or two, perhaps rounding up shoals of small fish into knots that can be attacked with mouth agape. You will remember that Ron Borlase caught the record Chew brownie at dawn with a Worm-fly in very shallow water. The boat angler rarely has a chance for these great brutes.

My preference is for bank fishing, even though I do appreciate the odd day afloat. Bank fishing gives me the opportunity to throw a long line, which I enjoy. I also have the opportunity of solving casting problems in adverse wind conditions, whereas the boat always drifts before the wind. There are other factors. I soon become very restless in a boat and long to stretch my legs. If I am wading, I can come out of the water whenever I like to have a doze without having to consider anyone else. Again, if the weather is unpleasant, I prefer to be ashore, for I find nothing more disagreeable than enduring the heavy rain in an open boat.

The speed at which you fish your flies from a boat is often determined by the drift, and the same applies to the depth at which they can be worked. The bank angler is able to get far more variety of depth, speed, and motion in the working of his flies.

Before moving on to the methods of boat fishing, I should like to discuss what I can only describe as "boat manners". There is nothing that so enrages a bank angler as a good wash surging through his area. Because most boat fishermen cast a short line of some 10 to 12 yards, they seem to have no conception of the distance that the bank angler is hitting. Many times boats have actually passed over the water being searched by my flies. Since they have the entire reservoir at their disposal, including the deep water in front of the dam where wading is naturally forbidden, the bank angler has every right to expect to be left in peace. The other aspect of this is when the boatmen decide to come ashore for some purpose. They seem to think that there is no harm in landing between two bank fishermen who are just a few yards apart.

On one occasion, a single angler in a boat hooked a trout which dived to the bottom. He was in two minds whether to play the trout or control the boat which was being spun round in a brisk breeze. Eventually he lost the fish and wound up aground where three anglers were fishing together. Fortunately, they were too amused to be angry.

You can always recognise the expert boat anglers. They cast alternately to avoid tangling with their partner's line. They do not stand up in the boat and crash around on the boards in heavy boots. Standing up in a boat in order to cast may be downright dangerous for an inexperienced person, besides which the rocking movement he is bound to impart to the boat will put down the trout. There is no marginal advantage in throwing a long line from a boat. It is better to fall into a smooth rhythm based on about twelve yards, which can be fished out by a left-hand retrieve, followed by a lifting of the rod tip flowing smoothly into the next cast.

Although there seems to be no reason why a boat should not be anchored, the usual practice is to row well up-wind, and then drift back with the boat sideways on to the flow. It is to gain the advantage of covering a wider expanse of water. Boat anglers often prefer to drift along one of the slicks of water that is distinctively marked by the wind, though there seems to be no logical reason why fish should prefer to lie in these streaks. These tactics are the elementary facts of boat-fishing, and, to be frank, it is possible for those with little or no previous experience of fly-fishing to make a respectable catch.

It is my experience, boat fishermen are far from imaginative in their choice of fly. It boils down to a team of traditional lake-fly patterns, or else the local favourites. I have rarely known them to attempt to match insects upon which the trout were feeding. I believe this is both due to the fact that adequate baskets are taken in this way; also that the flies must be worked in accordance with the speed of the drift, rather than by the choice of the anglers.

One summer's day, my wife and I were boat-fishing on

Chew, and near to us were a number of other boats. I could hear the choice of fly being discussed. These other anglers were fishing with teams of standard flies, including the inevitable Worm-fly, and we were doing the same during that part of the day when there was no sign of hatching insect or feeding activity. In the early evening, the air became heavy, first with Chironomids, locally called Buzzers, and then with larger cinnamon-coloured sedges. By matching the natural flies, we were able to make a nice haul, while the others persevered with their standard teams and caught nothing because the fish were preoccupied with food-forms that they easily recognised in the water.

This example of one-upmanship demonstrates that boat anglers would be advised to copy the fly on or in the water, rather than flog away in desperation. When I first fished Weir Wood lake, the popular choice was a Peter Ross on the point, a Mallard and Claret as the middle dropper, and a Rough Olive as the bob-fly. The cast would be prepared before arriving at the water, and attached to the reel-line no matter what conditions were prevailing. Most anglers consider the Peter Ross to be a fry-imitation, and as such it should be worked at a faster speed than the other two copies of insects.

Of course, this sort of fishing does bring its reward through sheer persistence, but it is as dull as ditchwater. Just watch a couple of anglers fishing a drift. They cast monotonously in front of themselves, drawing the team back across the water, then rowing back up the lake to repeat the performance.

The first consideration is the speed of the drift. A newcomer to the sport may not allow for this. Casting his flies in front, he does not realise that he is rapidly overtaking them, and even though he is recovering line, they may still be lying motionless in the water. Then, while he is struggling to cope with the next cast, the hooks are under the boat and fast in the planking. This is why it is important to use a drogue for windy days to reduce the speed of the drift. It is always best to cast a short line on a fast drift, fishing it out by raising the rod-tip into the first movement of the next cast.

The rate of the drift is important for another reason. When fish are neither feeding on the surface nor near it, the flies will not have time to work down to them. The alternative is to fish a long, sunk line behind the boat. It is not necessary to throw a long line, for it can be paid out behind the boat, but in the deeper holes, 25 to 30 yards must be fed into the water before the lures can be made to bump the bottom. The retrieve is now much slower, for the speed of the drift is added to the rate of retrieve. I find that a Black Lure is most effective for these conditions, and you may occasionally come to grips with one of the huge trout that have switched to a fish-only diet.

This stratagem of fishing a lure behind the boat introduces a problem of ethics. Strictly speaking, this is not trailing, since the line is both paid out and then recovered. Yet there is little doubt that a lot of trailing is done. Bank anglers tend to sneer at those who row continuously round the lake with their flies swimming in the water behind the boat. Regulations vary from place to place, but in general, I do not frown upon the practice while the anglers are rowing up to commence a drift. After all, there is little fun in it, and one could as easily buy fish at the fishmonger.

The most frustrating conditions of boat-fishing are those of hot, bright, sunny days when the surface of the water is as still as glass. The boat makes little or no progress; it is in fact, becalmed. Yet, there is often one small area where a feeble air current strikes the surface and causes a slight ripple. I believe that this may be due to the displacement of air on either side of a rising thermal, that column of warmth and moisture sucked up from the land by the sun. Thermals are easily detected by the sight of birds, particularly swallows, which feed on the insects that are carried ever upwards by the ascending air. Be that as it may, it is always worth while seeking any slightly troubled water which will help to conceal the glitter of the cast and the wake of the knots.

When there is absolutely no respite from the heat, my companion and I have a set routine. One of us will sink his line as deeply as possible, while the other will fish a greased line and cast with tiny nymphs gently twitched in the surface film.

It is no consolation to recall that the greatest brownie I ever hooked—and lost—latched on to my Peter Ross under such conditions. This, too, was on Chew lake, and I was so dispirited by the deadly calm that I had not troubled to change the relatively large flies that I was fishing during the windier morning. Indeed, I was feeling so sleepy that I was casting and retrieving in the most desultory fashion. The trout snatched at the fly by the side of the boat, catapulted into the air, and fell back a free fish. For a fraction of a second, while he was at the zenith of his leap, we looked at each other. I still carry an indelible image of a monstrous trout with a beautifully small head and golden flanks sprinkled with vivid, scarlet spots.

In normal weather, it is still a problem to decide upon a team of wet flies from a boat. I content myself with the following simple rules. If there is no sign of fish feeding on hatching dayflies, and if there is sufficient direct light to be reflected by their tinselled bodies, I will mount a set of three "flashers", such as Peter Ross, Alexandra and Dunkeld, thus mixing gold and silver flash in the same team. In dull conditions, or in pale, diffused sunlight, I believe that fur or wool-bodied flies will provide an attractive silhouette, more so than the slim flashers. This is when I fall back on the well-proven favourites, Mallard and Claret, Woodcock and Green, or March Brown. In no type of fly-fishing do I accept the ancient dictum of "bright fly on a dull day, dull fly on a bright day" for it seems that each sort of fly will be exposed to the conditions of light least favourable to it.

Choice of fly is simplified by the presence of insect life or fry activity and feeding fish; this is being discussed in later chapters. It is no great trick to operate in midge and sedge hatches with copies of those insects. Local anglers will know the life of their water. They will anticipate certain patterns of trout behaviour by the time of year. Sometimes the visiting angler can guess the reason for the success of a local fly, when the habitués just know that it is a good fly. This working back to the insect was done in the case of the Amber Nymph, a Bristol favourite which resembles the sedge larva.

You will have guessed that I am not a great lover of boat fishing. It is altogether too automatic. I must concede that the thinking angler can improve the standard technique. One variation is to work the flies diagonally across the wavelets instead of dead ahead. Weighted flies can also provide a variation in depth. But the boat-angler still does not enjoy the wide range of tactics open to the bank angler, nor does he encounter the same number of problems.

Boat angling has its uses. It is a fine nursery for beginners, for they should be able to bag a few fish in the early stages of the fly-fishing apprenticeship, which is a great incentive. It is also a painless way of introducing wives to the art, for a little understanding on the Home Front means a more appetising lunch basket on the next trip. And it is equally good training for youngsters not yet strong enough to throw a long line from the bank.

There are also some lakes and reservoirs where unrestricted spinning and bubble-float fishing have frightened the fish to keep well away from the normal limits of fly-casting. Here, again, the boat fly-fisherman is able to compete on less favourable terms than his brother on the bank.

Yet, despite the advantages that the boatman has, in being able to use lighter rods and lines, in being able to reach far-out fish without effort, bank fishing remains my first love.

CHAPTER IV

APPROACH TO BANK FISHING

WHEN YOU consider the effects of the wind on a large reservoir, you realise how inapt is the term "Still Water". The water is never still, even in light airs, let alone when it is being driven by a stiff breeze. The rules on most of our day-ticket reservoirs allow fishing officially from one hour before sunrise to one hour after sunset. I must confess that this rule is rarely adhered to by angler or authority, and I believe that "from first light to a little after dark" would be a more realistic description of the real situation. Providing that the ban on actual night-fishing is applied to prevent poaching, I see little fault in the rule as liberally interpreted by the anglers. I am drawing attention to this fact for an altogether different reason. I want to drive it home at the outset how many hours the fisherman will be working for his supper, but, in passing, it also brings out the tremendous value for money the bank angler enjoys.

It is true that occasional criticism is levelled at the charge of a pound or two, but in comparison to a day at the seaside. or even on Hampstead Heath, the price is fair. Bank facilities are invariably excellent, with toilets, shelters and litter bins being provided at intervals along the bank. Besides this, there is the traditional anglers' hut, where tackle emergencies can be met, records consulted, and a wash and brush up is available. Finally, there are the wardens to restock the lake, trap the coarse fish, and catch the poachers. Where could you buy more for a pound?

If I digress it is to pass tribute to a great band of friends that I have rarely had time to chat to on the bank, for there was always a trout showing out there.

The hours of casting and the wind have a direct relationship to each other. Nowadays I have a routine before every angling trip, no matter what species I am after. I adopted this as a consequence of taking up boat-fishing at sea. Not being a robust sailor, I find it imperative to sort out the weather conditions by telephoning the weather-forecast service before setting out. In reservoir fishing, if the direction and force of the wind can be ascertained in advance, it can be mapped on a chart of the water so that a position can be chosen in theory. This is vital, for the first few hours of daylight may be windless, and although I believe in the value of casting along a lee shore, punching out into the eye of a gale is most exhausting. An adverse high wind can spring up during the morning, and this elementary precaution can save you a tramp of several miles in waders to the most favourable bank opposite.

The technique of pushing a line into the wind is well worth mastering, for, although it may sound paradoxical, it does seem as if you can throw a line under the wind. This apparent absurdity is accomplished by delaying the forward line-shoot as long as possible, then cutting down hard with the rod-tip. The line bowls out low to the water, the flies curving smartly downwards into the waves when the leader is fully extended.

The effect of wind and waves on the line and flies should be counteracted. For example, a brisk breeze against you will sink your flies quickly, and deep. Your line will more easily become submerged. The speed of the retrieve must be increased to neutralise the results of the wind-driven current, for otherwise there would be a risk of striking on slack line when a trout seized one of the flies. The power of the wind's force upon a large mass of water is considerable. A stiff blow from right behind your back will flatter your casting, but the flies will sink with difficulty. They must be retrieved more slowly to prevent them from skidding on the surface, a fault you may not see yourself on the broken surface. Occasional attention to the leader with soap-solution will assist sinking. In summer time, a wind from behind may be bringing up very cold water from the lower layer of a deep lake. This will make the windward shore less fruitful.

With the modern floating lines, a problem arises when casting across a strong wind. The line will form a bow, and the flies will behave in much the same way to those cast down and across a river. They will swing across with the "current" with some speed, and then hang limply in the water. When the line is curved, it is difficult to keep in touch with the flies. Striking is again a problem. The line should be mended to keep it reasonably straight, and the flies worked more slowly when they are being dragged sideways by the pressure of the water.

If you do have to cope with a wind blowing from straight ahead, it will tend to drive the flies into the ground behind you on the back cast. Adjustment has to be made to the application of power, putting less steam into the first movement of the cast in order to give the line a real punch into the air current on the forward throw. On occasions, when the wind rises to gale force, there seems to be little alternative other than chucking in the towel altogether. Few of us like departing fishless on those precious free moments when we can go to a trout lake, even if there seems to be but slender chances of making a kill under such vicious conditions. There is a freakish quality of squally winds of which you can take advantage. It often blows fitfully, and it is possible to time your casts by waiting for the relatively quieter moments between the fiercer gusts.

To be honest, I never despair of fishing under these conditions. Often the trout are compelled into the coffee-coloured water under the lee-shore. I shorten the cast to one of 7 feet with a heavy belly, and I cast a single, large dull fly on a short line, retrieving it smartly. The idea is to create the impression of a tiny fish that has been bewildered and stunned in the commotion. The best fly I know to achieve this illusion is Ivens' Green and Brown Nymph, for a "flasher" such as the Jersey Herd would find precious little light to reflect in the suspended mud on the lee-shore. We must rely on outline.

An anorak is protection against the wayward fly being swept off course, and I also wear a pair of clear eyeshields for the same reason. If a gusty wind springs up suddenly from a sky full of cumulus clouds, you should expect rain, for you are probably in the "nose of the squall". This is cold air being dragged down with the rain and then spreading out in advance of the shower in a shallow belt along the ground. In hilly country, you may have longer to wait, as this air seems to flow down the hill-sides for longer distances.

A wind sweeping along the shore from left to right is a boon to the long-casting right-handed angler, for the fly is carried away from his body on the forward throw. A wind from the opposite direction can be an absolute menace. The flies are carried behind the head before the forward movement has begun, and the hooks may lodge dangerously in the neck or ear. The solution is to cast in the shape of a letter U, as seen from above, the nearer stroke of the cast being made on the back-cast, the further one on the forward cast. This takes the flies further away from the head.

Later on, I shall discuss the length and type of leader in relation to individual tactics, but it is also important to carry different lengths for weather and wind conditions. These would range from the knotless taper for calm conditions to the short, heavy leader for the near-gale. Under normal conditions, anglers find out for themselves the length of leader which they can manage. My own average between 10 and 12 feet. I prefer to suit the thickness of the leader to the combination of three factors, the weather conditions, the size of the fly, and the weight of the fish, but it is often hard to strike a balance. Except in very still water, our reservoir trout do not appear to be "gut-shy", so it is wise to err on the side of safety.

Besides the physical problems of casting into the wind, it is important to bear in mind the effect that it has on fish and the food they rely upon. It is not too fantastic to suppose that all types of weak-swimming creatures will be forced under the lee-shore, and followed by the trout. The clay being eroded from the bank will reveal more insects. Contrariwise, I have never given credence to the theory that fish will anticipate the terrestial flies born by the wind from the trees to the water under the windward bank. I can support the idea of fish following an insect migration visually in the water, and I know they pursue the crowded watersnail pilgrimages that happen from time to time. I believe that they locate most of their food by immediate reaction to happenings in or on the water, but I consider the idea of anticipation endows them with more powers than their brains have.

Since the war, a more scientific attitude has crept into all branches of angling. Richard Walker in his classic book on still-water angling and Worthington and Macan in their book on life in lakes and rivers in the New Natuarlist series, all stressed the importance of the division of deep lakes into two layers of water of widely differing temperatures during the summer. The top layer, of course, is considerably warmer than the lower one. However, when the days shorten, the warmer layer loses heat by night-time radiation, and then the Autumn gales mix the two layers together at a uniform temperature. This Autumn overturn probably comes to some of those trout lakes that close their fishing late in October, but this subject has been so expertly ventilated by the authorities I have quoted that it would be tedious to repeat it here.

It is important, though, to think of this before choosing which bank to fish from. Some lakes will have baylets that will always provide choice of wind direction, but that whole side of the reservoir will be affected by the tilting of the upper warm layer. The warmer surface water piling up on the lee shore will be more friendly to the fish and it will contain the tiny food-creatures borne there by forces against which they are too weak to struggle. Some anglers go so far as to carry thermometers to measure the temperature in different places, but for the fly-fisherman, this is going to an unnecessary extreme. The difference in temperature is so marked that it can be felt immediately. Even on a steamy, summer's day, I have been fishing with a light breeze behind me, and I have been shocked at how icy the water felt when I plunged my hand into the ripples. I think this helps to explain the phenomenon of fish being caught in the margins in the early morning, when it is often windless, only to disappear in an hour or two. Perhaps a wind has sprung up, tilted the warm water away from that particular bank, and covered the area with bitter-cold water from the deeps of the lake.

There has been an unfortunate image of the bank angler built up in the minds of those who do not fish reservoirs. It should not be necessary to waste words to refute the foolish charges of snobbery. Affluence is as widely spread as education, and people wisely will choose those sports that have always given pleasure to those with the means to pursue them. Fly-fishing is restricted rather by lack of space than wealth. Yet the charge persists, and is often repeated in the columns of the angling press. Of course critics have a right to air their prejudices, but they keep alive the outdated idea of the fly-fisherman being a tweedy snob. In fact many coarse fishermen, especially matchmen, spend more money on their fishing than do most fly-fishermen. I know a day at sea for Cod costs me more than a day at Blagdon or Chew.

The solution would be to conduct these critics along the banks of a reservoir so that they could meet fly-fishermen from all walks of life. I was delighted to read a letter by a foundryman in the *Angling Times* in which he rebuked these inverted snobs.

Another charge is far more serious. It boils down to the allegation that the average bank fly-fisherman is an unintelligent oaf who plunges straight into the water, scaring every trout for miles, and then he indulges in pointless casting to the maximum of his effort. One such critic used the expression "bone-headed athleticism" to describe this day-dream. It is largely to answer such ill-conceived spleen that this book has been written, for constructive ideas are the best answer to destructive comment. This does not mean to say that many bank anglers do not derive tremendous satisfaction from being able to reach a trout rising at 40 yards distance. It is a skill demanding a great sense of timing, and I wonder if there is a whiff of sour grapeshot in the strictures against it.

I must confess that the purely mechanical aspects of fly-fishing interest me but little. I try to master the secrets of double-haul for a purpose, to deliver the fly. The cast is far from being an end in itself. For myself, and, I am sure, the vast majority of reservoir fishers, once a satisfactory standard of casting has been gained, we perform the functions without preoccupation. We concentrate on the trout and how to deceive them. The behaviour and choice of fly becomes the obsession.

These critics are continually putting up their own skittles in order to have the pleasure of knocking them down again. We are supposed to have tame, hand-fed trout that rush up to take the fly and give themselves up without a fight. I wonder if the stock-pond bred carp behaves in such a gentlemanly way? I know that the first scorching rush of a Chew trout dispels this fatuous idea, but how can you convince an angler who has never hooked them? We know our quarry is both wary and game.

The casting routine outlined in chapter one is designed to give distance without great effort. The reservoir angler knows that although he may have the chance to catch trout moving close inshore at certain times, there are other occasions, such as when buzzers are hatching in deep water, when his casting ability will spell the difference between success and failure.

Fly-fishermen vary in temperament, as do all anglers. Some will be content to stay in a single position and catch what comes along. Others will roam along the banks, looking for signs of rising fish. One man will keep changing his flies, while another will be happy with a lucky favourite. I believe that it is better to work to theories, even if they are wrong on occasion, for they will provide the basis of a system of fishing. One step in improving morale is to eliminate indecision on the one hand, and blind persistence on the other. This is the purpose of planned tactics.

It is convenient now to discuss striking and playing of trout in still water. Although there are occasions which call for some delicacy, such as when a fish rises to a fly on a short line, or when you are using flies on small hooks, such as in a hatch of caenis, generally speaking, fish will take large hooks at quite considerable distances. If you have made up a shooting head, the elasticity of the monofilament running line has to be taken into consideration. This means that the stream-fisher's turn of the wrist is useless. The strike must be a full-blooded upwards sweep of the rod.

Timing is another question where river experience might lead you astray. The traditional "God-save-the-Queen" pause is no use, for the very distance of the line itself will often more than compensate for this pause. I find that I have been too late to hit fish that I struck immediately I felt them. Sometimes we are fishing deep, and the only indication of a take will be a lifting of the line at the point where it disappears into the water. Strike! At other times there will be a swift savage pull to which your reaction will feel an hour too late. Either way, the fish will either be "on" or "off" straightaway. Even when dry-fly fishing on reservoirs, I find it best to strike as soon as I see the rise.

There is another curiosity of lake fishing. Without the current of a river to act against the line, a rise to your fly on, or near the surface may be seen but not felt. These signs should all be struck, swirls, bulges, or head-and-tail rises towards the end of your line. All the same, there is nothing more frustrating than to see a trout boil at your fly, and then, on striking, to find that you have not hooked the trout. We all know this misfortune as a trout that "came short". The inference is that something aroused the suspicions of the fish at the very moment of taking the fly, thus making the rise-form near it, deceiving you into believing that your fly had been accepted. Another classic description is of the fish tweaking the tail whisks of the fly in playfulness.

The fly-fisherman's art does not hinge on the cunning of his opponent. Obviously precautions have to be taken in approaching a wary quarry, but this is true of all hunted and hunters. It is a question of instinct that even the simplest of creatures inherit. The purpose of the artificial fly is to imitate a food-form in such a way as to provoke the feeding reflex of the fish, for it is no more than a reflex.

It is also apparent that when trout are feeding exclusively on one particular type of insect, then a reasonable copy of that food must be offered. If the trout did not have any mental powers other than a purely instinctive reaction to environment, it would be almost impossible to catch them on the artificial fly.

If the idea of the intellectual trout is ruled out, the problem of the short-riser remains. It must be remembered that the trout in still water can approach the fly from any direction, and by the laws of chance, it is possible to strike at the same angle as the cruising fish, literally pulling the fly out of his mouth.

Downstream wet-fly fishermen have always recognised this danger, and salmon anglers throw a loop of line to a taking fish below them to ensure that the hook is tugged home into the scissors when it returns to its lie. In lake fishing, we must try to discern the line of travel and strike in the opposite direction. More often than not, a feeding lake trout is working up against the wind.

New factors also creep in with distance casting. I have cast a dry-fly into a ripple so far out that I have not been able to see it. It was necessary to strike at each rise. More often than not I discovered that the trout were picking off the naturals near to my own artificial. These fish might have been classed as "short-risers".

It is possible for the hook to glance harmlessly off bone or cartilage without the ghost of an impact, and although this is unavoidable, attention must be given to hook-points and barbs. I once fished near to an angler who missed three trout before he bothered to check his hook. He found to his chagrin that he had lost the point on the pebbles behind.

Equally important is the angle at which a fly swims. This is linked to the art of fly-tying and the aim should be to centralise the hackle below the hook shank to form a keel, while the wing above acts as a stabilising vane. If this wing is twisted or not straight from head to tail, the fly will skew in the water and fish in an unnatural manner.

We can only conjecture about the angle of the fish's direction when struck. Presumably it is diving, perhaps turning, which accounts for the hook, normally swimming upright, twisting and lodging in the "scissors", which is where I usually hook trout on the wet-fly. I take great care to see that my flies work correctly when drawn through the water. A lop-sided hackle or wing can be cured surgically with nail scissors, but it does emphasise the importance of anglers learning to dress their own.

Playing out lake trout does not present us with such problems. True, they make strong runs, usually out into the body of the lake, but unless there is a heavy weed growth, the angler need exert no side pressure. I suppose a greater proportion of hooked reservoir fish come safely to the net than other species in various waters. Yet the angler should be aware of any snags, for you can be sure the fish will. The ruins of great trees and sunken fences and ditches will be the chief hazards. But this is all common sense.

Where I do disagree with many anglers is in the idea that because the water is vast and clear and the fish strong and fresh, he should be allowed to run under light pressure until he becomes exhausted. This is the basis of the wide reel and extensive backing. I feel there is far more danger of a long, heavy line in the water dragging free the hook than there would be in a sharper contest on a shorter line in which the full power of the rod would come into play. Even trout of 4 lbs in prime condition have been played out on my 9-foot

Two Lakes fly-rod without running out the splice of the ordinary 30-yard double-taper line.

A danger does occur with a fish that takes to the air on a taut line, and though I believe it to be a sensible precaution to lower the rod-tip, in practice my reactions are woefully slow, at least for the first leap. This often happens as soon as the trout feels the iron strike home, and catches me by surprise.

Experience dictates different ways of playing a fish. Some will play them right out before netting, while others will prefer to bustle them in quickly in case too much thrashing on the surface will tear loose the hook hold. I prefer the tougher approach. When I have an assistant to net a "goer", I prefer to come ashore and control him from some way up the bank, with my friend crouching low to avoid alarming him at the crucial moment.

One thing remains to be said. Please unhook undersized trout gently in the water, and kill the good ones quickly and cleanly. A tough opponent deserves your respect. Undersized fish need not be handled. Most of them can be safely freed by running the fingers down the leader to take hold of the fly. A vigorous shake releases the trout without damage.

At this stage, it is wise to consider the problem of knots. It is now accepted that the only safe way of joining two lengths of nylon is with a blood-knot. My own experience is that nylon should be knotted while absolutely dry. When the step-down of thickness from one length to another is considerable, I put an extra turn of the thinner nylon into the knot. In fact, this works out at three turns of the thicker monofilament to four of the finer, which balances up the knot. Another precaution I take is never to cut the loose ends flush to the knot, but to leave the slightest fraction protruding to take up any slack in the coils during working practice. After a while, blood-knots are quickly tied at the water's edge, but for the newcomer to the sport, it is of assistance if a needle is placed in the fly-vice to keep open the gap through which the ends must be tucked back. Finally, the coils are snugged down on top of each other with the fingernails, and

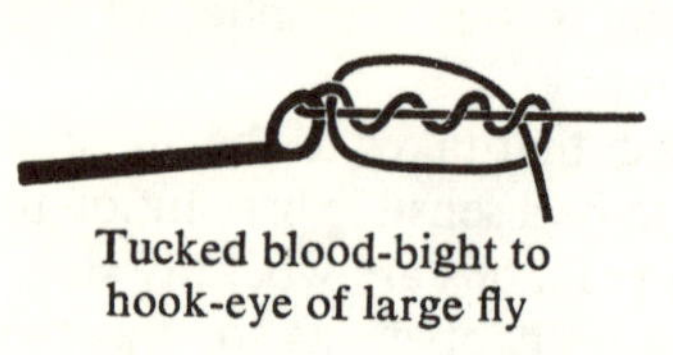

Tucked blood-bight to hook-eye of large fly

Turle knot to ditto small fly

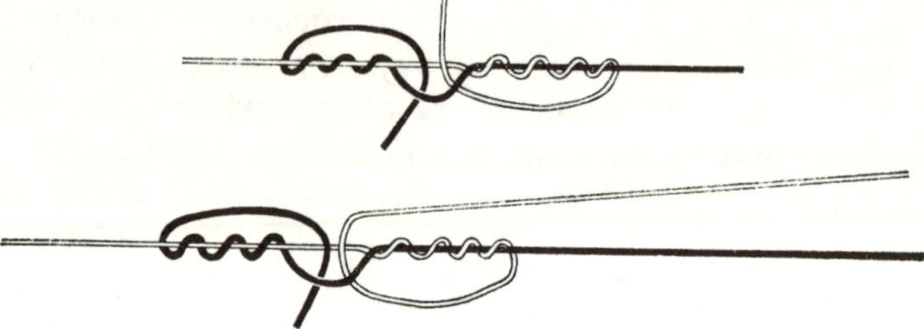

Blood-knot for joining lengths of nylon of various thickness, 3 turns on thick nylon, 4 on thin, and ends not cut too flush

Ditto, leaving top loose end uncut for about 4 inches for a fly-dropper

Blood loop for the end of the nylon cast, and ditto being joined to line by figure-of-eight knot, with a single granny in end of line to prevent slip. N.B. I describe the use of a needle when tying the blood-knot to keep the middle loop open

the knot given a steady pressure as a test.

I also prefer the blood-loop for the butt-end of the leader, for the ordinary overhand loop, though quite safe, throws the leader into an angle to the loop. The blood-loop keeps them in the same plane. I have never been let down by the figure-of-eight knot to attach the line to the loop of the leader, and it does allow speedy changes to be made. Never forget to make a granny knot in the final end of the line to prevent slip.

There are some mild arguments about which knot is the most efficient for the attachment of the hook. Of all the links in the chain, this is the one that most frequently fails, due to the fact that this is both the finest part of the tapered leader, and the most subject to strain. There have been some complicated inventions, but, as far as hooks down to size 12 (Old Scale) are concerned, I use a tucked blood-bight. In some books I have noticed that it is thought sufficient to make three turns of the nylon, and then simply turn the loose end back through the gap next to the hook's eye. I consider this to be insufficient, and I tuck the end back through the top turn of the knot, and leave a fraction protruding on cutting off the spare end. Some American anglers even go so far as to touch this end with a cigarette to form a blob less likely to pull back through the knot.

One morning at Blagdon, a friend and I found the trout taking quite freely, but for every trout I brought to the net he lost one, complete with hook. On investigation, it was revealed that I had tucked back the end of my blood-bight, while he had not. His knots were slipping, and I suggest you perform an experiment. Tie the simple knot that he used, soak it well, and then subject it to a hard strain. I think you will find that it will slip. Then, tuck the end back as I have described, and try again. You will learn what made the difference on that particular morning.

The blood-bight has another advantage. It allows the hook to "hinge" freely. My favourite knot for tiny flies lacks this quality, but the blood-bight would be too obtrusive. I use the Turle knot on these smaller hooks, but they do hold the fly quite rigidly. In a dry-fly this is an advantage, for it assists the fly to alight correctly on the surface of the water.

I must add a footnote about leaders. Of course you will select a length suitable to conditions, and the thickness of the point will be appropriate to the hook-size. In his book on still-water fly fishing, T. C. Ivens gives an excellent selection of double-tapered leaders for long-casting from the bank. I believe that these directions are somewhat over-precise. It is scarcely necessary to use numerous lengths of nylon of 12 to 18 inches, for such a number of blood-knots will cause too much surface disturbance. Having decided the length of leader, together with the thickness of the point, I make it up in about four lengths of nylon, stepping it up to stiff butt. In the long leaders, I tie in a heavy belly of nylon of about 20 to 22 lbs b.s. in the middle. This helps the nylon to turn over at the end of a long cast.

It is futile to lay down the number of flies to fix to a leader, for it will depend entirely on the tactics. I know an angler who regularly uses 10 to 12 at a time, while others are content with a single fly. I usually attach my droppers to extensions of the thicker, upper lengths of nylon of the blood-knot. There is little risk of this pulling the knot undone, providing that it has been tied correctly, and the opposite end not cut off too closely.

In these introspective days, no book is complete without some words on morale. Food, the right clothing for the prevailing conditions, these are obvious essentials. I am not competent to comment on the psychology of fishing. So much depends on the temperament of the individual. I am rather an anti-social angler, and I am not very keen to indulge in aimless chatting with passing anglers, so I will confine my remarks to more physical aspects of morale.

Tackle and tactics may be perfect. The other vital ingredient is concentration. The trouble on still water is that this concentration must be keyed up for long periods. If your attention wanders, you start pondering about matters at home or work, or you begin to admire the sunset, those are the very moments that the trout swirls at the fly. Concentration is likely to fade away with fatigue. Not only do I advocate rests during the day, but they should be timed to leave you fresh for the fruitful times of the day.

I have suggested ways of reducing tiredness, by careful choice of position, by falling into an easy casting rhythm. The rest is common sense based on the rules of normal activity, food, warmth and sleep.

A still-water trout is in the bag and its happy captor smiles in relief!

The author casting in squally conditions

A massive rainbow taken by the author in April 1973

CHAPTER V

CATCHING THE "STICKLEBACKER"

A DEFINITION is called for. A "sticklebacker" is a trout that is feeding on small fish, perhaps minnows or the fry of other species, such as perch, which are numerous in many of our reservoirs. Another term is often bandied about in fishing circles, the "cannibal trout". This is supposed to be a huge, ugly brute that feeds exclusively on other fish, and never rises to the fly. I hope to dispose of this legend as far as lake trout are concerned. The trouble is that many anglers believe that a trout freely takes fly up to a certain size, and then becomes "cannibal". On some waters this becomes the excuse to introduce bait-fishing and spinning. I wonder that the fishermen who do this are never amazed at the great quantity of immature trout that they destroy by these means.

Now the "cannibal" must be fitted into his proper perspective. The truth is that all trout are predatory from their early days. When just a few inches long, they will pursue fry eagerly, and consume them. They also become cannibal, and do not distinguish tiny trout from other fry. This habit does not alter throughout their lives. It may be true that older trout rely more on a diet of fish than insect protein, but it is completely untrue that such fish will not fall to the fly-rod, since we know that many of our artificials are copies of small fish.

I have been unable to bring to light any reliable data about the proportions of fish-food to insect enjoyed by lake trout, but I believe that on many of our reservoirs the "sticklebacks" are the bread-and-butter of existence, and the insects and flies are the goodies. It may be beneficial that certain numbers of coarse fish dwell in our lakes to replenish the trout's larder with their progeny.

Nor should this disturb the fly-fisherman, for there is no more versatile instrument in the hands of a competent angler than the fly-rod. In spinning, it is the engines that call the tune, and variety in depth and speed is largely determined by the mechanics of the business. The fly-fisherman dictates these factors to his flies by his own skill. In short, he can take trout that are feeding on fry and minnow. It is because of this, plus the belief in the importance of the "stickleback" in the trout's diet that I have promoted the tactics of dealing with the problem to first place in this book.

There is nothing that so exasperates the lake angler as a day of "sticklebacking". The water seems to be black with fry, which scatter in frenzy as the arrowing attacks of the hunters are seen on the surface, ending in the angry swirls as the assault is driven home. At such times, the artificial fly is virtually ignored. One such morning, the trout were herding the minnows along the Whalley Bank at Chew. Two neighbouring anglers climbed on to the concrete slipway to peer into the water.

"There are millions of them!" I heard one exclaim, and shortly afterwards they drifted disconsolately away to seek for a place where there would be no signs of trout in a feeding frenzy, and their flies would be conspicuous in the water due to an absence of other food. The correct approach would have been to fish the right fly in the right way, for it was surely the right place.

I have made no meticulous study of the habits of these small fish, which I shall refer to collectively as minnows. I do know that in cold water they drop down to the lake floor. In sunny weather, they rise to very near the surface, and in some lakes are recognisable as dark patches. They are often sheltering along the fronds of weed beds. I have had swarms of them darting among my waders at Blagdon, right in the marginal shallows. Another important fact is the change of colour when the male minnows adopt their courting dress in May. Their reddish-gold waistcoats are well simulated by the Jersey Herd fly. But otherwise these minnows are rather drab, and appear to be a splotchy, pale brown on top, fading away to a white belly.

Early in the season, or when it is particularly cold and grey, there will be no surface commotion to indicate the activities of sticklebackers. Yet it is a sound bet that the trout will be searching them out along any deep trenches near to the bank, especially where the bottom shelves away suddenly, or, in rather new reservoirs, where ditches or lanes plunge into the lake. This is the time for the sunken, "wet-cel" type of line and the weighted lure.

It is common practice for anglers to strip these minnow-lures back as fast as they can pull the line. If you watch minnows in the water, you will see that their characteristic movements are short, swift darts, with rests between them. I do not believe in the long, rapid left-hand pull of the line on recovery, but prefer a series of jerky tugs of about 6 inches at a time to make the fly follow minnow behaviour.

When you are using a shooting-head with a running line of 18 lbs b.s. nylon, you will find it hard to do the figure-of-eight bunching of line in the left hand when you retrieve your flies. Instead, you will have to let the nylon fall into the water at your feet, unless you use a line-raft. Incidentally, before you start fishing with the shooting head, run out a length of nylon along the bank, and have a friend give it a good stretch. This helps to overcome the springy effect of the material that would otherwise cause it to form into coils for a while.

It is on warm, summer days that you can really come to grips with the stickleback raiders, and their forays seem to reach a pitch of intensity in August and September. Trout harrying the fry near the surface will often break the water, which can mislead you into believing that they are rising to fly. The signs to watch for are the needle-marks of the scattering tiddlers, the V-wave of the trout's back, and the untidy disturbance of the surface in comparison to the usual neat rise-form to natural flies.

Sometimes you will notice a "sticklebacker" on a regular beat, but on other occasions, two or three fish will make vicious raids right into the shallows. The signs may be apparent in the early morning, so it would be foolish to plunge straight into the water. I have caught these bandits by keeping well away from the edge of the lake, kneeling or taking advantage of any cover in order to make a "cross-country" cast into the shallows. It does no harm for the line to lie across the intervening dry land, and it is always more logical to go after a visibly active fish than to search the water at random. I always prospect along the banks for signs of these trout, for I expect them to turn up on the leeward shore, even if deep water is not to be found. Once the first party of wading anglers churn up the shallows, the opportunity is over.

It is an education to witness two or three huge trout beating up a weed-bed for minnows. One or two of them appear to hurl themselves into the weeds to drive out the cowering refugees, while the others scuttle round the outside, mopping up the fugitives that attempt to escape. I have seen this happening for a whole afternoon, yet the culprits are very hard to catch.

It must be driven home that this minnow-feeding is a preoccupied habit, not just a casual binge. The trout know what they want, and they are not going to be tempted by any other offering. It is obvious that an artificial must be used to copy a small fish. Instinct dictates an Alexandra or a Jersey Herd, but these, too, often fail. I reiterate that tinsel-bodied flies depend for their success on the reflection of direct light. They can be quite successful in bright sunlight, but once the source of direct light is removed, they become mere outlines, and outlines which are wrong as minnow imitations. An artificial is needed for dull conditions, diffused sunlight, early mornings and evenings, and cloudy water. The best that I know is Ivens' Green and Brown nymph. Pull one through a shoal of minnows and you will see that it virtually becomes one of them.

The size of the minnow-fly is as equally important. A glance at the shoal reveals that many of the minnows will be from upwards of an inch long. If this is tied on an ordinary iron, we have a salmon fly. Indeed, the early record books from Blagdon, as well as the mounted fish on the walls of the fishing hut there, prove that such lures were most killing in the past. It is not a pleasant hook to cast and drive home, but happily modern ideas have given us the tube fly. One rewarding experience came as a consequence of an exchange of ideas on reservoir trouting with James Gilmour, in which I sent him some samples of flies that I use for minnow imitations. Being quite formidable by normal "loch" standards, he scaled them down. One day, under most adverse conditions, he took a brownie over two pounds in weight, which was a magnificent fish for this water in Renfrew. The emphasis was on tactics related to the conditions and behaviour of the trout, rather than on tradition or unrelated local habits of fishing.

The Green and Brown Nymph is easily dressed. The body is of alternate turns of green and brown ostrich herl ribbed with narrow gold tinsel. The tail is a few strands of peacock herl, which are brought over the body to form the back. They are then twirled together to be wound together round the hook near to the eye to make a small head. If you have no minnowish fly in your box, a good tip is to take any large fly, such as an Invicta or a March Brown, and cut off the wing and hackle. It may well work.

It should also be remembered that, except in cold weather, the trout will be driving the minnows up towards the surface. This is plainly deduced from the commotion. It is a bright idea to grease the leader to the final foot, and draw the fly slowly in front of the charging trout. The artificial seems to collect a knot of minnows, who elect it as gang leader and follow it. The raider is attracted by this exciting target. When he charges, they all scatter—except your's.

Tactics begin at the fly-dresser's bench, which is why I briefly described the fundamentals of preparing artificials in chapter two. I wish to encourage the reservoir fly-fisherman to follow up the subject on his own initiative, for it would be outside the scope of this book to treat the art extensively. Nevertheless, fly-dressing is married to the progress of this book at every stage. Cast your mind back to the elementary processes I outlined earlier.

Amateur fly-dressers evolve individual styles as they progress. The characteristics of certain well-known dressers are immediately recognisable, as if each of their products bore a trade-mark. Flies made in workshops to standard formulae are usually indistinguishable, one from another.

Personal style does more than show off the eccentricities of its author. Style is introduced to serve the innovator's scheming to catch more fish, often by promoting new techniques within the framework of traditional fly-fishing. A fine example has been cited in the Ivens' range of flies. Style can also be introduced into standard patterns to the extent of creating a tailored fly that will beat its unmodified brother as a trout catcher.

Of the standard patterns, the most effective fry-imitator that I know of is the Peter Ross. Its silver body, gill-like red dubbing and scaly-back effect of the barred teal wings simulate convincingly a darting tiddler. The aim of style is to enhance this effect.

The Peter Ross is not an easy fly to dress, since six different materials must be fixed to the hook shank, and this can cause bunching around the hook-eye. Teal, like Mallard, is a difficult feather for winging, since the barred feathers tend to twist and split when being pulled down to the shank by the tying thread. Our first aim should be to simplify the dressing.

There are only two ways of introducing style into a standard pattern. Firstly, it is to change the materials, and secondly to vary the methods of dressing. In other words, the colour and outline of the fly can be varied to achieve special effects. The behaviour of the fly in the water depends on whether it has soft or stiff hackles, long or short wings of feather or hair.

The traditional Peter Ross has a body of which the lower

two-thirds is silver tinsel and the top third is red seal's fur. The whole of this body is ribbed with oval silver tinsel to increase the flash. To simplify and increase the glitter of the body, I replace the dubbing with teased-out fluorescent wool, and I use a lurex tinsel for the body, ribbing up over the wool. The tippet tail and black hackle are the same as in the standard fly, but the wings are the most important factor in giving outline to an artificial. Since our Peter Ross must appear in minnowish guise, I tie in full, long and well-rounded teal slips to give this effect.

The advantages of the tube-fly for minnow imitation have already been mentioned, but I stress the right length, the more substantial body and the better hooking qualities of a small treble hook compared to the rank point and barb of a normal hook of the same length. Tubes may be purchased in different weights and lengths. The heavy ones are of metal, lined with polythene, and are admirably suited for cold-water and sunk-line. At the other end of the scale are delicate plastic tubes of half an inch, two of which can be used end-to-end if required.

The tubes are simplicity to dress. My own method is to fix a darning needle into the vice and to slide the tube firmly on to it. Thread is wound on in the same way, leaving enough room for the head. Although salmon anglers attach hair and hackle to the head of the tube, our minnow of green and brown ostrich herl needs no such adornment, but is prepared in exactly the same way as if it were on a normal hook, except that the "back" is left out, for it is impossible to determine at which angle the tube will swim in the water.

One tiny irritation about tube flies is the tendency for the treble to ride at an angle to the body, or even to snarl up the leader on casting. John Veniard recommends that a small sleeve of valve rubber be slipped on the butt of the tube into which the eye of the treble should be pulled. Alternatively, a small slot can be filed into the tube-end, and the hook-eye pulled into that.

To summarise my minnow campaign, I use three tube flies, weighted and unweighted, for all conditions. Firstly, there is the Green and Brown, as described. Secondly, there is my tube version of the Jersey Herd, the body of which consists of gold lurex, with a tuft of orange goat's hair in place of the hackle, and the usual peacock head. A silver-bodied alternative of this completes my armoury. I like the tubes to be about an inch long, and the trebles are No. 14's. A little silk padding in the middle of the tube gives it a minnow outline.

My parthian shot is this. Do remember that the fly is more effective if presented at an angle to the trout's vision. You can hardly expect him to chase a flying treble hook.

CHAPTER VI

THE MYSTERIOUS BUZZERS

I BELIEVE in many reservoirs, minnows and worms are the staple diet of the trout. Yet they also feed extensively on insects. The river fly-fisherman, on turning to still-water, is tempted to think in terms of dayflies, the group of insects known scientifically as Ephemeroptera. Where possible in this book, I shall prefer to employ the angler's terms rather than the scientist's. Dayflies such as the Olives are not so important in trout lakés, for it is the family of flies that the entomologists have named Chironomidae that are most prolific and widely distributed. The fisherman's names for this group varies from place to place in the British Isles, Blae and Blacks, Duck Flies, Midges, and Gnats are all common. But I have chosen to discuss them under the heading of "Buzzers", the name by which they are recognised on the Bristol lakes.

Like many an angler, I turned to reservoir fishing after serving an apprenticeship on rather meagre rain-fed streams. One fresh experience used to irritate me to the point of vexation. This was my inexplicable failure to gain advantage from the evening rise. The sun slowly sinking in the West was accompanied by a lessening of the wind, until either the surface of the water was gently ruffled by a slight breath of air, or else it became as hard and black as ebony. Then, far off, I would hear a "plop", then another near at hand. Eventually, my eyes would discern a trout head-and-tailing within casting distance. Feverishly a team of wet-flies would be driven out to intercept his line. There would be no "take". Before I had made a few more efforts, the rise would be into its stride, increasing in momentum until the lake was on the boil. Perhaps there would be a handful of sedges dipping on the water, yet rarely would a copy be successful. This frustrating experience might have been repeated over and over again, except that a passing angler commented during one of my numberless fly-changes, "I see that they are well on the buzzer tonight."

Buzzers develop from eggs laid along the surface in chains of jelly. They become the larvae that are familiar to all owners of old-fashioned water butts, for some of them will be our friend, the Bloodworm. Apart from these, so called by their red colour, others will appear to be transparent worms of an amber hue. The red coloration is that same haemoglobin that carries the oxygen round our bodies, but in the case of the buzzer larvae, it acts more of a storehouse of oxygen to enable it to exist in tiny tunnels in the mud in the deepest part of the lake.

This partly explains the flies hatching at a distance from the shore in the deep water, as well as spelling out the need for the angler to be able to throw the long line which arouses the jealous scorn of his critics. I will pause at this stage in the creature's life cycle to point out that although the larvae are not considered worth imitating, there is no doubt that bottom-feeding trout seek them out with avidity. When there are no indications of trout activity, it is well worth the experiment of fishing a team of larvae copies, very slowly, and right on the bottom of some of those deep holes that lie not far from the bank.

These are two tyings with which I have taken the odd fish. They should be dressed on long shanked hooks. These hooks are covered with a layer of fluorescent material, preferably floss, slightly thicker at the head. Colours indicated are bright red, greeny-yellow, amber. This undercoat is evenly lapped over with fine clear nylon or horsehair to give a segmented effect. A few fluorescent fibres can be tied in at the tail, and a turn of similarly coloured herl with a short flue at the head, but more for attraction than imitation.

The single drawback to this fly is in the rigidity of the body, for the natural worms are always twisting themselves up into all sorts of contortions. You only need to glance into that water-butt! The purist may experiment with detached bodies made from flexible materials, such as nylon, suitably dyed or dressed, and attached to the hook in various imaginative postures. One thing is certain; this is a too important food item to neglect, even if only as a long shot on a dour day. In due course, the time varying from species to species, the larvae pupate, and make their way up to the surface, where they are suspended under the film for a moment or two prior to emerging as the perfect adult fly. At this stage they are most vulnerable. If the hatch is sufficiently widespread, it produces a general rise, such as I have described, but, even on a small scale, it may produce a local rise of trout. A hatch of these buzzers may take place quite early in the season, building up to the prolific emergences of the flies in the Spring and Summer.

The buzzers seem to start hatching in isolated places in the early afternoon, and I often shoulder my rod after lunch to go prospecting for a local trout reaction. But as the emergence swings into its stride, the flies are moving off the water to gather over the bankside vegetation, and sometimes the clouds of whirling buzzers will be intensive and dense. In the evening, the females will be returning to the water to lay their eggs and die off, when the dry-fly is propitous. The life cycle recommences.

It would be a happy coincidence if the various families of buzzers resembled each other as closely as Olives. Alas, they do not. They vary considerably in size and colour, and the trout so preoccupy themselves with the current hatch that they will select unerringly the appropriate size and colour of artificial from among a team of three. If you should be unlucky enough to mistake the popular favourite, your hopes will be slender.

At Blagdon, a friend and I usually mount a team of three buzzer nymphs, black, green and red. One evening last June, we both took some trout on the black fly, the colour that seems to predominate. After a pause of inactivity, the trout came back to the flies, this time selecting the green pattern. On both occasions we noticed natural buzzers of the favourite colour hatching out and skimming away across the water. Often, the darkest flies will emerge earlier in the day than the lighter ones, though this is not an invariable rule.

It is a good idea to catch the local specimens in order to match their size and colour. Mostly the fish will be interested in the bigger flies, those that can be imitated on hook sizes 12 to 16. Having confirmed the size and colour, it remains to note carefully the shape, so that these details may be reproduced at the vice. The wings are small in relation to the body in the adult fly, and they point backwards in repose. The body itself is segmented, and the tip of it is hooked downwards. These characteristics point to a body material of formed-in coils, such as nylon or horsehair. If a flat material is chosen, such as floss silk, it must be closely ribbed with a fine tinsel.

If horsehair or nylon is used, a wad of wool or fur must be dubbed in to form the bulky thorax, but in the latter case, the turns of silk should be built up to copy the thorax and hump of the wing cases. A few turns of herl, dyed to match the body, completes the artificial.

I am a firm disciple of the modest application of fluorescence in artificial flies. Since many of these patterns will be employed during the evening, a modicum of D.F.M. material should be infiltrated into the dressing. I have suggested a fluorescent underbody to the horsehair, and one or two teased-out filaments in the woollen thorax might lend enchantment to the trout's view. Of course, there is no possibility of fluorescence with the black artificial, but with the green and red buzzers, the body will have a wonderful translucency, while the thorax sparkles with points of fire. It seems that trout may be susceptible to the "purkinge shift", which means that they are sensitive to light rays at the blue end of the spectrum. It seems certain that they have a different range of colours to us, and from time to time we are made aware of these variations, such as when G. E. M. Skues found the

Orange Quill to be a deadly fly during a hatch of Blue-winged Olives. It suffices to say that as the light weakens in the evening, we want to capture and reflect as much of it as possible in the dressing of our fly. Fluorescence achieves this.

There is one pattern of fly that I must add to the armoury, and that is the "Footballer". To the best of my knowledge I originated the fly, though, since anglers often think about similar problems at the same time, unknown to each other, I make no positive claim. It is intended as a copy of the buzzer larva hanging in the surface film. The body is of alternate turns of black and white horsehair, started well round the hook bend, as all buzzer body materials should be, and the thorax is of mole's fur, followed by a head of peacock. It is a good pattern to try in the early afternoon when there may be a local hatch of darker buzzers.

During normal buzzer activity, it is a good plan to mount a team of three or four flies of different colours, and a 14 hook is a sensible compromise to begin with. This is greased-leader fishing, for the flies should only hang an inch or two below the surface on short droppers. Since these pupae are but feeble creatures, the flies must be worked very gently. If the trout start picking out the same coloured fly on the team, I do not switch the other flies for others of similar colour, for later hatches of buzzers will probably be of different hue, probably lighter.

As the evening draws down, the female adult flies will be hovering over the lake on their egg-laying mission. At this time, a combination of the nymph and dry-fly can prove deadly. The simplest way to dress the dry buzzer is to add a cock's hackle the same colour as the dressing. Perfectionists may tie in a pair of hackle-point wings sloping backwards along the body. White or honey are suitable colours for these.

The evening rise is such an obvious manifestation that it will be obvious where to fish, although the bank angler would be wise to station himself at a point where deep water can be reached within comfortable casting distance. I have discussed both minnow and buzzer imitations, and how to use them, but I can relate them in an incident from my reminiscences. There is a corner of Blagdon where a gut of deep water lies between the bank and a large weed bed. The vegetation must flourish on an area of the lake floor that rises in the bay, and its edge is some 30 yards distant from the nearest casting position.

During the afternoon, my companion and I were attracted by two or three hefty trout beating up the weeds for minnows. Since we were both using light rods and orthodox lines, the furious shaking of the fronds and surface uproar was at the utmost limit of our abilities. But time and time again we dropped minnowish flies right into the commotion without the ghost of a pull. We were both soon exhausted, and had shipped water into our waders to try to gain a few precious inches. The shooting-head and double-haul technique would have overcome this strain, but, at that time, we had not experimented with these ideas.

Towards five in the afternoon, the minnow gorging ceased. A few minutes later, there was a sporadic rise to some dark buzzers that were breaking from the deep gut of water. We changed to teams of buzzer nymphs, and shortly my friend connected with a fine brownie of 3 lbs. Sure enough, it was choked with minnows.

The casual prospector in the forenoon may well be able to stalk a fish rising to a premature, limited hatch. I have only twice taken sizeable trout with consecutive casts, and one of these occasions was the result of such an expedition, also at Blagdon. I had strolled nearly right round the lake on a calm, hot afternoon, when I noticed slight dimples on the surface in front of a marginal weed-bed. One or two buzzers were bursting from their pupa-cases and skidding off drunkenly towards the trees. I greased the knotless tapered leader to the last six inches, and fished a small Black and Peacock Spider through the area. Almost immediately, I felt a tug, and bent into a 2 lbs rainbow. I netted him, cast to the same place and caught his twin brother.

For the angler who is unable to dress his own flies and has

to rely on shop patterns, the following standard flies may be standbys: Black Spider, Black and Peacock Spider, Blae and Black, for dark buzzers. For red and green buzzers, the wings and hackles can be cut from such patterns as Woodcock and Green, Teal and Red.

The vital aspect of the buzzers is their universal distribution. They should never be neglected on Scottish lochs. Were a more exact copy used than a small wet-fly, such as the popular Blae and Black, then I am sure the dividends would be richer. This was another fruitful issue from the exchange of ideas that I had with James Gilmour, for he had previously fashioned a nymph, to which I added my "footballer", and the results during one season on his local lochs around Paisley were astonishing. I am certain that Welsh lakes would similarly unlock their hearts to the buzzer. The lessons we have learnt from the reservoirs are applicable to any tract of still water in the land, provided that it holds trout.

CHAPTER VII

THE IMPORTANCE OF SEDGE-FLIES

THE STREAM fisherman will find that I am still the heretic, for I rate the sedge family as being of more importance to the trout in most still water than the Dayflies. These flies, also called caddis-flies, belong to the order called Trichoptera, but most anglers will be familiar with the term "sedges", and recognise them when they appear. Their life story resembles that of the buzzers insofar as the egg changes to a larva, and then a pupa before the adult, perfect fly takes wing.

I have avowed before that the fly-fisherman should rationalise his system of flies. This is borne out by the fact that C. F. Walker, in his treatise *Lake Flies and their Imitation* states that there exists 189 British species, most of which care little whether they operate in still or running water. Many of these are too small to interest the trout, while another group are only of local distribution. Of the remainder, there are some which the trout do not seem to relish, even though they may hatch in great profusion from a lake.

One such sedge-fly used to mystify me at Blagdon. It was small and inky, and it used to appear in large numbers during the early afternoon, and by late evening the bankside bushes would all wear dark halos. Yet only on rare occasions did I ever see a trout take one of them. I went so far as to create an imitation, but that, too, proved useless.

I must return to the life history of the sedge-fly, for just as the trout appreciates feeding on his favourite insects at all stages of their development, so too should the angler learn to profit by this habit. For too long we have been confined to being satisfied only with copies of the flies that we could see.

Fortunately, writers such as C. F. Walker have changed that state of affairs.

The sedge larvae which we know so well are those that construct little homes for themselves out of small particles of wood or stone. These are greatly liked by the trout, and post-mortems have often revealed traces of these cases in the stomach of the fish. Bait fishermen on some streams winkle the larvae out of their refuges and use them on their hooks. This, together with the baiting with the larvae of the stone-fly, is called "creeper fishing" in some places, though logically it should only be applied to the latter.

When I was very young, it was my delight to collect these caddis cases, for I had a biology teacher who encouraged his pupils to bring to school all kinds of revolting curiosities, though I remember that grass snakes and toads were the popular favourites. I could never understand how the sedge larva kept his home together, until I learned that he first makes an inner tube of a sticky substance produced by glands in his mouth. The bits and pieces that form the outer shell simply stick to this substance, which then sets. The larva is still most selective in choosing the bricks for his outer defences. He does not merely roll in the nearest rubbish. It seems that different species of sedge will choose material of a certain type. The well-known angling entomologist Martin E. Mosely, was most impressed with the speed with which the newly hatched larva would set up his home. Observations in his laboratory showed that newly-born grubs had constructed perfectly formed cases from fine grains of sand within 24 hours.

Some species of sedge larvae do make these homes for themselves, but seek shelter in aquatic plants or under stones. It is logical to assume that as the larvae are valuable to the bait fisherman, then a copy of them should be exploited by the fly-fisherman. Up to the time that C. F. Walker produced his book, no conscious effort had been made to design such a pattern. Walker found sufficient numbers of the caseless larvae in the stomach contents of trout that he decided to fill the vacuum himself, which artificial, being described in his excellent treatise, is not repeated here.

However, for a number of years, fishermen at Chew and Blagdon have been reaping much success with a fly known as the Amber nymph, though no one seems to know the reason why. It seems very probable that this artificial is a reasonable copy of the sedge larva. John Veniard attributes its invention to Dr. Bell. The tying is as follows. Body—amber floss silk or seal's fur tied rather thick. Thorax—brown floss silk or tur, approximately occupying one-third of the body. Wing-case—a strip of any grey-brown feather, tied in at the tail and finished behind the thorax. Hackle—a few fibres of pale, honey hen, tied in under the head and extending backwards.

To render this fly effective as a copy of the sedge larva, it should have an undercoat of 5-amp fuse wire, so that it can be sunk deeply along the edge of the weed beds. It must be worked very slowly. I also work into the body material a few fibres of fluorescent wool.

We should not despair of imitating the larva in his case. A judicious searching with the net, or even an autopsy on the trout should indicate the favourite material for the house. Some of these larvae may be as long as three-quarters of an inch, so a long-shanked hook makes a fine starting point. The hook is lapped with the fine wire, and an underbody formed of floss silk, with a turn or two of clipped cock's hackle followed by a head of brown herl. The body is coated with cellulose varnish to which the fragments of wood, or grains of sand are attached while it is still tacky. This copies the larva in his case with head protruding. I have held trout so gorged with watersnail that they can be rattled, so these cases are chicken-feed to them. I suggest this experiment as a long shot when fishing is slack.

It is probably the pupae that are most vulnerable to trout attack, a stage which many sedge-flies reach after a year of feeding on plant and animal material. The case-bearing larvae have no problems about making their cocoons, for they only need to plug up the end of the tubes, but the free larvae have to indulge in a lot of spinning to make a shelter of a hard, silky substance on the side of some underwater object. Every maggot fisherman will be familiar with the idea of a cocoon containing a pupa, for this is similar to the chrysalis stage of the gentle, or "casters" as these effective baits are called by Northern match anglers. The maggot angler will also remember of that occasion when he neglected to empty away his supply, and left the tin with the lid on for a few days. When he next opened it, the bluebottles came shooting out like bullets.

When the pupa has developed inside its cocoon, it rips open the covering and emerges in form very similar to the adult fly that it will become. This explains the effectiveness of wet sedge-flies, as well as successful patterns like the Invicta or Woodcock and Yellow. You often see these sedge pupae breaking to the surface of open water, where they hatch, but other species swim to the shore to prepare for the next stage. It is true that C. F. Walker has invented some most ingenious copies, both of the pupa and the emerging fly. For myself, I have found two trusty flies from the traditionalist to cope with both of these conditions.

For the pupa, my favourite dressing is that invented by Ronalds many years ago. It has stood the test of time. It also has the virtue of simplicity. The body is given as fawn-coloured floss silk, but it is a wise precaution to dress some hooks with a darker brown silk to suit any local variation of species. The hackle is ginger hen, tied below the hook in the customary wet-fly position. And the wings are from a hen's wing, chosen to match the body, and put on flat, or rolled. I prepare a number on hook sizes 12 and 14, the darker dressings being on the smaller shanks.

I know that there are special dressings for the hatching sedge, that stage of the insect's life when it is breaking free from its jacket, but, so to speak, has not yet pulled its arms from its sleeves of the old coat. But, for me, there is only one fly to deal with this situation, and that is the Invicta. I would like to examine this further, because of its importance as a lake pattern.

I was instructing a friend in certain aspects of fly-dressing, and we decided to unravel the secrets of preparing an Invicta, for it is not one of the easiest flies to fashion. Examine the standard formula, which is given as:

Body—Seal's fur, dyed yellow ribbed with gold twist.
Body hackle—Red cock's hackle carried down the body, palmerwise.
Shoulder hackle—Red cock, with a few turns of blue jay.
Wings—Hen Pheasant tail feather.
Tail—Golden Pheasant crest.

Excluding the hook and the tying thread, there are seven different materials involved, some of them, like the jay's hackle and the hen pheasant wing-slips, being particularly difficult to manipulate. No wonder John Veniard says that salmon flies are easier to dress than trout flies! It will be obvious that the Invicta cannot avoid being a bulky fly, though this is not a drawback if we consider that the hatching sedge also resembles a miniature haystack. The dresser has to ensure that the hook point is not masked by a wad of fibres that might hinder penetration.

My friend regarded this array of materials with some dismay. "Is it really worth it?" he asked. Study the fly's pedigree before I pass on to solve some of the problems involved in its dressing.

The Invicta was invented by the great Cheltenham dresser, James Ogden, who was himself the son of a renowned angler, Frank Ogden. I regard Frank Ogden as the founder of the imitative school that eventually attained such a high degree of influence under the guidance of the Old Master, F. M. Halford. James learned fly-dressing at his father's knee, and with it he absorbed the principle of imitating the natural fly on the water, rather than churning out patterns to traditional prescriptions. This brings me straight back to the Invicta.

In dressing this fly, there is a problem right at the start.

How can we produce the cheeky, upturned curve to the Golden Pheasant crest feathers used as whisks? My method is to dampen them well with saliva, and let them adhere to the inside of a wine-glass. They will dry out overnight and retain this curve.

Next the ribbing is tied in, but why not use a modern lurex instead of the old-fashioned gold-twist? Then comes the yellow, seal's dubbing, but, remembering that the fly will be often worked hard in the weakening light of evening, some fluorescent yellow wool should be teased out and worked into the body material. When this is wound on, ample room must be left for the shoulder hackles and wings. The body hackle should be sparse enough to allow the wings to lie flat, and the lurex ribbing is wound up through this hackle to make it secure, then both are trimmed away.

Only a pinch of blue jay is needed with the red throat hackle. With larger flies, the stalk of the jay's hackle will have to be sliced to reduce its bulk and rigidity, but in small Invictas, I turn the fly upside down in the vice, and tie in a bouquet of the fibres. They can be held into a wet-fly position by turns of the thread. The bed of thread for the wings is built up far enough for two slim wings to lie snug to the body, and the fly is finished.

The bewildering army of materials has been blended into the fighting Invicta. I delight in the Heraldry of our art, but we must also preserve the practical purposes.

While the fly is taking shape in the vice, I am also miles away on a still, summer's evening. I can almost hear the beating of the tiny sedges' wings as they swarm and dip in their hundreds. Just below the surface of the lake the fly is swimming. The last rays of the dying sun slanting over the hills illuminate the body fibres with points of fire. The huge trout lunges, the rod bends and dances to the music of the reel. Can I hear James Ogden chuckling at his bench all those years ago? Glorious Invicta!

Having pupated and hatched, the mature flies leave the water for the surrounding land in order to mate, some time after which the females return again to lay their eggs. A word of caution must be injected here, for different species of sedge-fly will deposit their eggs in various ways. Some, like Silverhorns, are a delight to the dry-fly expert, for they fly over the water to drop their eggs on the surface. This habit, known as "dipping", makes them most vulnerable to attack, and when a large number of female silverhorns return to the water, it brings on a fruitful "rise".

A group of brown sedges crawl below the surface to lay their eggs underwater, others select bankside plants. The main problem facing the angler is in the large number of species with slightly different size and colour. Fortunately, they do resemble each other to enable the fly-fisherman to divide them into groups which can be copied by a single artificial.

I separate one sedge-fly from the rest, and I do prepare an individual pattern for it. This is the Brown Silverhorn, for although Courtney Williams, in his *Dictionary of Trout Flies* regards it as remarkable that "a fly which hovers over the water in such vast numbers should be so little liked by the trout", in my experience, a heavy hatch of Silverhorns is greatly relished by the fish, unless there is a simultaneous appearance of large quantities of buzzers. I do not think that the Black Silverhorn is half so popular as the brown one. Silverhorns are distinctive because of their long, striated antennae, as well as their habit of fluttering over the water in circles.

The Brown Silverhorn actually has a greenish body, which accounts for the occasional success of the artificial Grannom on reservoirs like Eye Brook, where it has a good reputation. The natural Grannom is one of the few sedges that only occurs in running water, but the artificial fly incorporates some green fur to indicate the egg-sac of the female. My own favourite fly for the Brown Silverhorn is similar to that listed by John Veniard in his *Fly-dressers' Guide*. The tie is:

Body—Dark green-olive tying silk.
Body hackle—Dark brown cock, ribbed with gold wire.
Wings—Waterhen (rolled).
Shoulder hackle—Dark brown cock.
Horns—Fibres of barred teal tied in at the head to a length twice that of the body.

One of the objects of this book is to select a range of artificials from the various systems that have been quoted and to match them to the tactics discussed. If all of these flies can be accommodated in one or two boxes, both selection and travel will be easier tasks.

The remaining species of sedge-flies are so numerous, and their differences so superficial, that I have found it convenient to class them under two headings, according to size. The larger flies are generally lighter in colour. These I copy with the Cinnamon Sedge pattern on a No. 12 hook, while the small, darker ones are dealt with on a No. 14 hook, the pattern being a version of the Little Dark Sedge.

The method of preparing these flies is quite standard. For the Cinnamon Sedge, I form the body from three or four fibres torn from the light ginger tail feathers of a turkey, while the body and shoulder hackles are of a similar colour of cock's neck. The body hackle should also be ribbed with gold wire, but my choice of wings is not usual, for I prefer to use the soft, mottled primary-feathers from an owl's wing. This feather is ideal for rolling, and it should be tied on top of the hook so that the divided sections extend well beyond the bend, just as wings of the natural fly, when in repose, continue further than the length of its body.

My Little Dark Sedge has a body of maroon silk, while the two hackles are of dark furnace. The perfect wing choice for many sedge patterns is Landrail, but since this is almost impossible to obtain, Waterhen is a suitable substitute. These are two patterns among many. If you consult Courtney Williams, you will find a large choice of well-tried flies from which you may pick one or two at random. Nevertheless, my own experience is that it is best to rationalise them down to a single fly for each of the two groups I have mentioned.

These flies will either be used as floaters, or to become bogged down in the surface film, where they are extraordinarily effective as imitations of the dead, or dying spent fly that has laid its eggs and completed its mission on earth. Although sedges appear early in the afternoon, and I have even provoked a rise by scattering them from the marginal vegetation, it is not until the sun drops down towards the horizon that the rise gains momentum. Normally the sedge-fly is opaque rather than translucent, and I am certain in my own mind that the correct silhouette is more important than colour. Although the fly's wings have not the dusty appearance of a moth's, they do have many tiny hairs. This is why a palmered hackle is not offensive, and the extra turns of the shoulder hackle assist the buoyancy of a fly that would normally sink readily because of the heavy quantity of wing that it carries.

The sedge-fly is the obvious flaw in the argument of those who emphasise the wet-fly approach. The intelligent angler is he who quickly adapts himself to changing conditions. Many times I would have been fishless if I had continued to ply a team of wet-flies when sedges were being hunted on the surface by eager trout. The question of tactics is often so simple that it is overlooked, and we are tempted to invent complex, even fantastic theories to account for our failure. If the trout are feeding on surface flies, that is where our own imitations of those flies should be.

I make one reservation about this. In my experience, if a simultaneous hatch of sedge and buzzer occurs, the trout may become preoccupied with the latter if it is there in large quantities. This can be misleading, for the sedges are obvious to the eye in the fading light, while the smaller, nippier buzzers may go undetected. If your sedge stays neglected in a heavy evening rise, this may be the explanation.

Although I have not come across the Silver Sedge in reservoir fishing, I do not regard the pattern as of much consequence, though some of my companions violently disagree. I am sure that the well-known artificial is intended to represent the Grey Flag, a sedge, which, like the Grannom, is confined to running water. However, it is easy enough to dress up one or two of the flies I have described with bodies formed of white silk or fur, ribbed with narrow silver tinsel. One advantage would be the ability to incorporate some fluorescence in the material, for in the darker colours used in my other sedge patterns, it would be pointless.

Because of the importance that I attach to the silhouette, I have no great faith in hackled flies. Neither do I like those winged with hair, for the amount often used for sedges is heavy enough to turn a fly on its side, or even upside down.

There is yet another sedge-fly that I must single out for individual attention. This is a fly that has been considerably neglected because of its size. The truth of the matter is that fly-fishermen must become accustomed to thinking of some of the larger insect denizens of our lakes. There is no doubt that Chew trout do not approach double-figures on a diet of mosquito larvae, even if they do relish them as an appetiser. And if the angler realises the importance of creatures as huge as the Dragon-fly and Damsel-fly, then the fly-dresser must satisfy his requirements. The one thing that trout have in common with humans is that they both seek the fattest reward for the minimum effort. The fly I am now introducing is the Great Red Sedge, or Murragh Fly, which is widely distributed, and appears to be most active in June. Some of the specimens that I have seen would not be the poorer for being compared to an artificial of one inch long; indeed, I have had grand sport with such imitations.

I usually do not "work" a dry sedge-fly on the surface. For one thing, sedges rarely become trapped in the film, as do moths. Their dipping is a temporary halt on the water's skin, and when spent, they are usually inert. Also, twitching or dragging a dry-sedge soon waterlogs it, causing it to sink. The one exception is the Great Red Sedge, which, when hatched on the surface, scuttles along the surface to the bank.

I am indebted to J. R. Harris for this word "scuttles" from his *An Angler's Entomology*, for I can think of no better description of the action the angler must imitate. I will describe it later on in the tactics for moths. I will merely add that this fly, fished at the right time and in the correct manner, will stir up a frenzy among the portliest trout of the lake.

I am equally appreciative of the pattern described by Mr. Harris for this largest sedge. I dress it on hooks as large as size 6, old scale, but due to the weight of the iron, I bind a sliver of cork or balsa to the underside of the hook-shank before the body is made. Harris offers a choice of body materials, dark-grey, black or black-claret mohair or seal's fur. I mix a portion of mole's fur into claret seal, which aids the dubbing to stick to the thread. Unlike Harris, I like to wind in one of the dark-red cock's hackles in a palmer fashion, securing it with fine gold wire. The remaining hackle of identical colour is wound in well at the throat, after rolled wings of dark-brown speckled hen have been attached to lie flat along the spine of the fly. As described in the section on moths, this pattern is a wake-fly and it has to be fully hackled to keep it afloat.

Bearing in mind that many summer evenings are calm, I prefer to fish the single dry sedge on a knotless taper from 11 to 12 feet in length. The hook sizes will necessitate a point of about 4 lbs b.s. Fishing with the dry sedge is one occasion when I like to abandon the long-casting shooting-head technique, and revert to a light dry-fly rod of about 9 feet and a double-taper floating line. If the sedges are prolific, distance will be no problem, for many trout will be moving well within range. Occasionally, I sweep through the rushes and reeds to drive the adult flies over the water; this is permissible groundbaiting!

It is always exciting to cast to rising fish. Normally, lake trout seem to move into the wind when on a feeding prowl, but when it is calm, it is hard to discern their direction. Few anglers seem to appreciate just how fast these trout may travel. It is true that sometimes a trout swims casually along, sipping down a morsel here, another there. Yet those three rises in a line, though occurring almost at once with a distance of several yards between them, may well be made by the same fish. The fly driven out to intercept his passage must allow for this.

I will not insult the reader's intelligence with arrowed charts of imaginary beats of sedging trout, but I have noticed that often they make sweeps in from deeper water, with a comparatively narrow arc near to the shore. It must be born in mind, that at this time on a popular reservoir, a long rank of fishermen will be hard at it. Have you ever noticed the extent of those ever-widening ripples breaking from the caster's legs? Each grunt of effort is accompanied by a violent muscular spasm down the entire body. On the quiet water, the effect is devastating.

There is one more problem of the dry-fly on still water. The upstream angler allows the current to bring his fly back to him, while he recovers the slack line in his left hand, ready for the next shoot. The reservoir man enjoys no such advantage. If he attempts to hoist the long line and fly from the surface at some considerable distance, it will result in a terrible strain on the rod, and the cast will be a disaster. If he retrieves the dry-fly across the surface of the water until he has a manageable line to lift, the fly will be soggy with water. The answer is to bowl a little hoop of line out across the water, and as soon as the fly shoots up into the air, a vigorous line haul with the left hand coincides with the back cast, to commence the next delivery.

Nevertheless, the floatability of the artificial is a reservoir difficulty, for with the extending of a long line, the mending to cure wind-drag, the fly will inevitably ship a bit of water. Besides this, our hooks should be of heavier metal than the stream fisher's to cope with the smashing takes that sometimes occur on still water. It is vital to procure good quality hackles. The use of longer, stiffer hackles cut back about halfway is also a trump card. I have previously mentioned the tying in of fine slivers of cork under the body dressing. What else can we do? Oily floatants are a curse on still water, for their oily sheen spreads far and wide, and I have never been impressed by the qualities of modern silicons. In older times, flies were soaked in paraffin and left to dry out before being used, a treatment that also deterred moths. John Veniard has suggested a modern version of this, whereby the hackles are steeped in a much-diluted cellulose varnish.

Looking back over the seasons, I recall that so many of my best rainbows and brownies have fallen to sedge that I am convinced that I am right in listing it so highly. Some of these trout have been hooked so closely to the bank that I doubt the wisdom of plunging into the water and thus disturbing the area. More and more, I find myself casting from dry-land when trout are sedging, even going so far as crawling behind bushes to stalk individual fish. I am sure that many chalk-stream fishermen would feel right at home during a rich hatch of sedge on a trout reservoir. But the exhortations of the wet-fly only school must be disregarded.

CHAPTER VIII

OLIVES AND THE OTHER DAYFLIES

THROUGHOUT THIS book I have mainly used fly-fishermen's names for the natural flies of our lakes. These are usually based on colour and size, though sedges and buzzers are exceptions. Sedges probably take their name from the bank-side vegetation where the adult flies often gather for mating. Buzzers are simply associated with the humming noise that they produce in company. It often happens that a swarm of these insects will collect around the boat-angler's head when he is rowing back to the landing stage at night. There is nothing very complicated about the recognition, naming and imitating the two groups of flies that I have introduced, but when we enter the world of Ephemeroptera, we are lost in a maze. Even the angler's classification of them as "dayflies" to distinguish them from the other two groups which are normally more prolific in the evening, this is a comparatively new term coined by C. F. Walker, but at least it is intelligible.

In the first place, previous experts have not always agreed about the labels of many of these flies. For instance, Walker did not agree with the name "Summer Mayfly" bestowed by J. R. Harris on a large species of dayfly by virtue of the fact that it resembles the well-known Mayfly, but is sensible enough to delay its arrival until later in the season. Walker proposes to baptise this insect the "Large Summer Dun". No doubt there exists a sound reason in logic for this change, and I imagine that angling entomologists derive harmless fun in their skirmishes about trivial details. But when this is applied to whole families of flies in their various stages of development, mere tacticians become confused by the welter of alternatives. Our object is elementary. It is to recognise the fly upon which the trout are feeding and copy it with a reasonable imitation and behaviour in or on the water. As in war, tactics may need to be executed with speed, for one two occasions I have witnessed good catches of trout during hatches of dayflies that were no more than of half-an-hour duration within a few square yards of water.

At this stage, it's worth considering in greater detail the problems of fishing the dry fly on still water. These "Dayflies" are far less important than keen entomologists would have us believe. True, local hatches occur, even dominate on rare occasions, but in comparison to sedge and buzzer, they occupy a mere fraction of trout diet on most waters. We must not attempt to translate chalk-stream philosophy to still water. Our dry fly-fishing, while of great value, shouldn't be based on the books of angling still-water entomology because their research, and the resulting emphasis, was carried out largely at smaller, unique lake-fisheries, like Two Lakes.

Having fished at Two Lakes very often, I can vouch for its richness and variety of insect life. Olives and Sepia Duns hatch profusely at times, yet on no reservoir have I seen a rich hatch of Sepias, nor preoccupied feeding response to it. We must be realistic, to think in terms of buzzers, sedges and various "terrestial" insects, in the main.

There are certain physical problems of fishing the dry fly on still water. Almost always we fish during a surface rise to floating or hatching insects. Not only must we be accurate in distance as well as direction, we have to be able to make rapid changes in distance and direction. The commonest cause of failure is that we fail to intercept the fish with the dry fly.

There are the usual options for fishing the floater, searching water at random, dapping and using a wake fly. Let us consider, though, true dry fly-fishing, which is the presentation of an imitation to deceive a rising fish. The rise is often sporadic, perhaps caused by small groups of cruising fish picking off the hatching olives in a small bay or it may be a widespread boiling of water to sedges on a summer evening. In any case, the natural insect will be clearly in evidence, on the water, in the air or by bankside vegetation. There will never be any doubt as to the right dry fly to use to match it. The only thing you could mistake is a sub-surface rise to buzzer pupae for a surface rise to floating fly, for the merest fraction of an inch separates the two.

Obviously, we use a lightish, responsive rod, like the "Two Lakes", which can lift a long line from the water and drive it in a new direction. The normal fly-line, with a fine-tip, such as the "Fast Taper" type can be rolled off quickly without drowning the fly. Glitter-free leaders should be prepared, with the nylon-surface rubbed down to a drab grey colour with fine abrasive powder, like "Vim". The fly being treated with floatant, the leader lightly greased, we're ready to go.

Many a dry-fly session has been spoiled by sheer eagerness. Relaxation and watchfulness are vital. Take a general look along a bank to see where the rise is strongest, such signs as clouds of fly, boils in the water, swooping martins or swallows, even bats, should guide us. We slip quietly into the water there, or if the rise is close, we find a point of vantage on the bank. Next, we pick up a more detailed picture of the rise. Probably the fish are scattered, but are they cruising along a bank, or circling in a tighter area? Try to work out the cruising direction of the feeding fish, either by the furrowing of the water by head and fins, or by the succession of rises. This should yield a "time and space" relationship.

The hardest thing is to put the fly exactly into the path of the trout, for the plane of the water is most deceiving. A fish apparently coming straight for the fly, may, in reality pass under the nylon or beyond the fly. Then, give yourself time. It's obviously a waste of time to put the fly into the circle of the rise, as the trout has gone. Gauge the speed of his feeding path, then put it well ahead of his beat, giving the fly and leader time to settle.

Of course, we can fish the rise at random, pushing the fly into the area of activity to wait for a trout to bump into it. This is successful during hectic rises but I prefer to go after a particular fish, sometimes even being able to choose the better specimen in an area of activity. Apart from this, there seems to be a psychological moment, just after the dry fly settles, when it looks its best, before subtle wind or water drag makes it appear in an unfly-like pose.

Now we have the inevitable question, to move the fly on the water, or not? There's no clear answer. Sometimes the fish will hit the fly only when it's motionless, at other times they want it to twitch or scuttle. Given that sedges are vigorous, moths struggle, small buzzers skate, there are evident choices then if the unmoved fly is refused. Olives, caenis and larger egg-laying buzzers when spent, are mostly quiet on the water. Chasing fish usually push their snouts through the surface film and zig-zag or furrow the water, and this spells out a clear message.

It is most difficult to evaluate the dry fly on still water. I can say with truth that it has caught many fish for me on days that otherwise would have been empty. I can add that it's probably the most enjoyable way of taking fish. During the old-fashioned "longbow" rod days it was condemned, but this may have been because anglers decided on a tackle system, then searched for fishing techniques to match it, whereas logic dictates the opposite course.

It may also be that still-water men hadn't mastered the art of relaxation. The trouble with a fine evening rise is that the atmosphere of excitement, even frenzy, communicates itself to the angler and the continual plugging away with wet flies, snatchily retrieved, matches the mood but rarely equals the hopeful expectancy. One has to bear down on one's nerves, no better way of doing which is to sit by the water's edge to gather data on the rise, as I've just described. It is the over-excitement which makes the inexperienced caster aim directly at the rise instead of computing where the fly should meet the fish next time.

Casting from a boat on a raw Spring day

A trout is struck at Two Lakes

The last gasp of a rainbow trout from Sundridge Lake

Finally, without doubt, different reservoirs have trout which move to the fly in various ways. At Grafham, a heavily hackled sedge, over-large in size, could be thrust out and smartly worked back on the surface, as a "wake fly", and this stirred up the trout even by day. Our fat, lazy fish at Sundridge would never chase anything, but requested the floater to be laid out before them, where it could be leisurely inspected and swallowed. At Two Lakes I found it far more successful to move the floating fly little, if at all, but at Coldingham, a Gread Red Sedge twitched along the surface could be very killing.

It is now necessary to introduce the actors. Unlike the flies we have so far encountered, dayflies pass through two adult stages, known in angling parlance as the Dun and the Spinner. Duns presumably take their name from their somewhat drab appearance when compared to the sparkling flies that emerge from this covering in full wedding dress. This final stage, the Spinner, is so called due to its rising and falling nuptial dance in the air, whereby it attracts its partner. Although Duns resemble each other sufficiently to be copied by a single artificial, the male and female Spinners may have completely contrasted body colours, which the perfectionist will copy. The Pond Olive is a fly that concerns the reservoir angler, and whereas the male Spinner is a rather dull grey in body, the lady glows with the colour of reddish-gold.

Before the adult fly breaks away from its shuck on the surface, it has already spent a good part of its life under the water as a nymph, where it is actively hunted by the trout, particularly when it is finding its way to the top to hatch. Generally, these nymphs resemble the colour of their duns, which explains why wet-fly imitations of the duns are accepted by the trout.

My object in this chapter is to avoid a danger, the pitfall of listing separately all of the lake dayflies, further dividing them into nymphs, duns, spinners and spent gnats and then to recommend separate artificials for each. C. F. Walker introduced seven artificial spinners, all of which I would have dealt with using a Pheasant Tail, should I have been lucky enough to have intercepted that rare event on still water, a fall of spinner heavy enough to stimulate a surface rise. He pictures five patterns of dun, where I would have been content to employ two, the Greenwell's Glory and the Blue Dun. Yet I imply no criticism of Commander Walker, for his book is a fascinating exercise in perfectionism.

The practical angler must reduce these dayflies into manageable groups, again for reasons of keeping the fly boxes and their contents to intelligible proportions. I am outlining my own methods of achieving this object.

I divide the dayfly duns into two groups, light and dark. The light dayfly duns are the flies to which I attach most importance, the Pond and Lake Olives, whose size and colour are closely alike. The remaining dayflies, those called variously Sepia and Claret Duns, I class as dark dayfly duns.

To simulate the nymphs, I use the Greenwell's Glory, for although it is now common practice to dress individual nymph-patterns, when these standard wet-flies are immersed in water, the wings cling to the body of the fly to create an impression of the "hump" caused by the thorax and wing-cases. The effective fly for the nymph of dark dayflies is the Mallard and Claret.

Halford referred to the Red Quill as the "sheet anchor" of the dry-fly fisherman on a strange river, and I know many anglers on still water who regard the Mallard and Claret in the same light. It is worth examining the structure of the fly in more detail.

The familiar dressing is given as:

Body—Dark claret seal's fur, ribbed with fine gold wire.
Hackle—Ginger cock.
Wings—Dark, bronze, barred Mallard.

Experience over decades indicates that anglers find the fly to be more attractive if the claret fur is darkened. I find it a good plan to work in a pinch of mole's fur to assist the seal's fibres to stick to the thread, and this also darkens the dubbing to the desired shade of near-black. The soft flank feathers of the Mallard are another of those fragile winging materials demanding much care in dressing. One way to form a stronger wing is to tie in double sections for the left and right wings, though this is wasteful at a time when these feathers are becoming scarcer.

Although I find hair-wings may unbalance a dry-fly, a tuft of fibres from the tail of a brown squirrel makes an excellent substitute for Mallard. Care must be taken to select only a narrow portion of barred hair, combing out the fluffy fibres at the base. I put a blob of cellulose varnish on to the bottom of the hair-wing section, then tie it in under the hook shank, level with the desired position. Then, as the thread is tightened, the hair is rolled into place with the fingers of the left hand. The Peter Ross can be similarly treated with hair chosen from the Grey Squirrel's tail, or, even more accurately, from a section of hair from the pelt of a Silver Baboon.

The Greenwell's Glory offers few problems. The body is of yellow tying silk, which, when well coated with brown cobbler's wax, turns to a dirty olive. The body is ribbed with fine, gold wire, and the hackle is Furnace Hen. I select wings freely from Starling, Coot or Waterhen; it matters little.

The importance of dayflies on rivers is so highly rated that many alternatives are offered to us. It is a question of confidence. The Rough Olive is a fly I like to use on the bob, while the Golden Olive is another attractive pattern. The Gold-ribbed Hare's Ear, dressed in the old style without the wings and hackle, but simply having the hair fibres picked out at the tail and throat, this is a killing copy of the hatching Olive when fished in the surface film.

Sooner or later, every fly-dresser decides to improve on tradition, and I am no exception. I give two dressings of my own which I have found effective for dayfly conditions. They are:

Light Dayfly Dun

Legs—Furnace hen.
Body—Greenish-yellow condor substitute.
Wings—Waterhen.

Dark Dayfly Dun

Legs—Dark furnace hen
Body—Dark brown condor substitute.
Wings—Grouse tail.

For general prospecting, I tie one of these patterns on the point, another on the dropper, and a Gold-ribbed Hare's Ear on the bob, thus making a systematic approach to all dayfly needs. I have found it to be an excellent boat team.

I must not leave this question of the nymphs and duns by creating the impression that I have little regard for them. Their value lies in the local hatches that occur in limited areas during the daytime, often from sunlit shallows at no great casting range. Little is to be gained by being rooted to the spot, hoping that the flies and the trout will find you. I love to wander along the more secluded banks, even along the very shallow reaches furthest from the dam, prospecting for signs of Olives. My heaviest Blagdon brownie succumbed to a size 12 Greenwell on a greased, knotless-taper leader fished on a light dry-fly rod. He swirled at the fly some ten yards from the bank, and took it barely an inch under the surface in about two feet of water. This was a hatch of only a few Olives that he was mopping up as they strove to the surface. I imagine that he was the only fish there.

A sequel to the story is that I dispatched the fly to a friend in Alabama as a souvenir. While crossing the Cahaba River, he heard it crying out for water. One fortnight after accounting for my big brownie in Somerset, it lit into a striped bass in America's Deep South. The Greenwell is quite a fly!

The curious aspect of the flies which I have been discussing, is that they so seldom inspire a general rise to the dun and spinner floating on the surface. Consequently, the dry artificials do not have the same potentiality as do the corresponding copies of buzzers and sedges. It is a pleasant experiment to try occasionally, perhaps when the arm is heavy. The Pheasant Tail, with its steely, light blue hackles and rich, red body, resembles many of the Spinners, and it is only necessary to tie in two darker blue hackle points to lie flat at right angles to the body, in order to produce a 'Spent Gnat'. This is the name given to the dead female after egg-laying, for day-flies, being unable to drink water in the Spinner stage, soon dry-up and expire.

Why do the trout neglect the floating Olives? The answer lies in the field of speculation. In still water, the nymphs may be so vulnerable while rising to the surface that the trout are occupied with easier pickings. That is my belief. It is strange that many anglers may not realise that there is a Mayfly hatch at Blagdon. I have frequently sat down to watch the nymphs shooting up from the bottom, to break open their nymphal shucks and fly away. The thing that amazed me was the speed at which the fly hatched, in a split second.

My observations on Kentish and Sussex streams, which have a fair hatch of Mayfly in spite of their poverty of other species, showed this to be a slower process. The stream fly takes some while to hoist itself from its shell, and, even then, the newly hatched Mayfly is too feeble to make an immediate dash for freedom, but drifts helplessly with the current while the wings harden. This is the basis of the "duffer's fortnight". But the Mayflies I watched at Blagdon burst forth and were away in a twinkling. Have the different conditions of still water given the hatching fly an advantage to compensate for the likely heavier casualty rate among nymphs? It is an interesting thought.

In any case, the odd Mayfly nymph or dry-fly, tucked away in a box in the breast-pocket, may be a shot-in-the-locker for a surprising appearance of this fly, as well as for the large Summer Mayfly later in the year.

CHAPTER IX

INSECTS FROM THE LAND

THERE ARE a number of tactics under this heading, so please refrain from asking "when is an insect not an insect". An important item of trout diet lies in a number of succulent creatures that are borne onto the water by the wind, or tumble into it accidentally from a tree. As they are out of their natural element, they usually struggle furiously, and the commotion attracts the cruising raider. This chapter is a peg on which I shall hang many hats.

You may think this introduction contradicts my earlier refusal to concede that fish have the powers of deduction and anticipation. I retract not one word. I do not believe that the trout will station himself under the tree in the expectation that grubs may fall. I do believe that he may see the arrival of the grubs, eat them, and wait for more. The former would be a reasoning process, whereas the latter is a reaction to environment. This is not idle speculation. It is vital to tactics that the trout is not anticipating the moth that blunders into the water, but that the ripples of the poor creature's vain attempts to free himself attract the fish.

If insects arrive from the land in sufficient numbers, they will probably bring about a rise in that vicinity. It is a situation for the dry-fly fisherman. It was once thought that wet-flies were accepted by the fish as duns or spinners that had been drowned and then were submerged. A glance at the debris along the lee shore soon reveals the fate of flies that die in the water. Those that are not eaten by fish, wash about on the surface until they disintegrate. Still water contains other predators than fish. A trapped fly is likely to fall victim to those insects that are designed for dealing with those in the surface film. It is a wonderful story of adaption, unfortunately outside the scope of this book, whereby the film acts as a giant web to insects that can travel in it to attack their prey. These predators value the surface film, and the fly-dresser and angler must never neglect it, for it is at that level that the trout sees these unhappy wayfarers.

The importance of moths was brought home to me some years ago. One evening, after a day of fruitless fishing at Weirwood, I was strolling along the top of the dam to the car park. For a moment or two I rested my elbows on the wall and stared gloomily across the darkening reservoir. The surface was as motionless as a mirror, although far out I could see the occasional splash of a rising trout, beyond the reach of the rank of bank fishermen I had left behind, still flogging away in desperation.

Then, just below the wall of the dam, a large brown moth flopped into the water, and his struggles to become airborn again sent ever widening ripples out over the deeps. There was an angry boil, and the moth vanished into the maw of a great trout. As the fish engulfed the fly, I saw him expose a golden flank. It was a far heavier trout than the trout we were normally catching at that time.

I determined then to investigate the possibilities of using moth imitations to catch trout on reservoirs, and I have had to submit to some ribaldry from my friends when I unwind a stout leader with my hefty concoction on the end. Because a moth is quite a sizeable mouthful for any fish, there is the opportunity of bringing up one of the hugest trout in the lake. Because of the limitations to the fly-fishing method to which we reservoir enthusiasts submit, some might be tempted to believe that specimen hunting is beyond the bounds of credibility. This is not true. Indeed, some of my tactics, such as attacking "sticklebackers", and the use of the artificial moth, are designed to deal with big trout.

I have found it a practical proposition to divide moths into two classes—large brown ones and small, light-coloured ones. Moth artificials are legion, and I will describe how to dress two patterns that have caught some bonny trout for me.

The first of these is an old favourite, the Hoolet, a very popular fly on Windermere. The hook must be enormous by trout standards. A size 6 (old scale), even with a long shank, is admirable, as is the equivalent fine-wire low-water salmon hook. A sliver of cork is bound to the underside of the shank and lapped with the underbody of silk to form a plump moth-like shape. This is covered evenly with six strands of peacock herl twirled together to create a fuzzy effect. A rolled wing from the primary wing-feather of an owl is tied in so that it is extended well beyond the hook-bend when divided. It is the aim of the dresser to make these wings lie flat, as in the natural moth. Finally, two large, brown hackles from a cockerel are wound in at the shoulder of the fly.

For the smaller, light moths I use hooks of sizes 8 to 10, with a thick body of white fluorescent wool ribbed with silver lurex. White, brown or mixed feathers are used for winging, and a white cock's hackle is wound in at the throat. Some natural moths do have traces of gay colours in their make-up. For example, one brown moth has orange underwings, and this can be suggested by a modicum of fluorescent wool worked in to the body material. I prefer to concentrate this bright shade towards the shoulder where the wings are fixed.

Of course moths are not designed to navigate on lakes, and when they blunder into the water, they swiftly bog down in the surface film. This is why I do not include an extra hackle tied in "palmer" fashion, as I would in my copy of the Great Red Sedge. This fly scuttles across the surface, so the palmer hackle hoists the artificial above the water's skin. I require my moths to settle down into this film and I rely upon my cork buoyancy tank to prevent it from sinking.

Courtney Williams lists several tried moth imitations. They are Brown Moth, Bustard, Ermine Moth (a hackle fly), White Moth and Hammond's adopted. I must also praise a New Zealand tying called Thompson's Moth, which, since it employs a cream chenille body as well as Brown Owl's wing, combines the advantages of my own two talismans in a single dressing.

How is the moth fished? Obviously it is deadly at the dusk of a Summer's day. Yet it takes courage to change from a sedge or buzzer nymph during a prolific evening rise. A leader should be prepared in advance, with the fly already attached, and this can be wound round the fishing hat in readiness. This leader need be only 8 feet long, but the point should be stout enough to suit the large hook and send home the rank point. I like to seek out some quiet baylet, preferably with deep water near to the banks and a barrier of rushes along the margin. I hate wading when fishing the moth, for I creep along behind the rushes, keeping a keen watch for patrolling trout.

All the rules in the book are broken! Short casts are made to these margin cruisers to avoid "lining" them. The big fly is thrown high into the air so that it lands with a healthy "plop". It must be retrieved in short jerks, the intention being to furrow the calm. The rises are usually vicious in which the fly is engulfed in a great swirl. The fish must be struck hard to drive home the big hook. You must really lean back heavily on the rod, simultaneously hauling line with the left hand.

Two points must be remembered in playing the surface raider. Sometimes the fish will be swooping in from deep water, and he brings in slack line with his own impetus as he continues to "run" on feeling the iron. Vigorous hand-lining is the remedy, for the loose coils at your feet may be recovered onto the reel when the fish is under control. When vast trout take a fly near to the bank, they may take to the air on being struck. The danger comes through a sudden strain being exerted on a short, tight line. Quick thinking is necessary to ease the pressure by a lowering of the rod-tip.

On one occasion, I was casting a moth to a trout that was casually wandering along the length of a miniature bay at Blagdon. His head and tail clearly marked his line of travel, but I muffed the cast. The moth splashed into his wake. Quick as a flash, he doubled back and I saw the V-wave arrowing straight for the fly, which I tugged an inch or two to add incentive. Then there came the exciting boil not more than six yards from where I was crouching behind the rushes. I struck, felt his weight before he bolted straight at me, with loose line tumbling down through the rod-rings. I lost contact and hand-lined furiously, until I regained touch with the fly now firmly and ironically stuck into the roots of the rushes at my feet.

The Daddy-long-legs is an ungainly brute. This accounts for its neglect by most writers in still-water fly-fishing. Ivens did not mention it, and C. F. Walker treated it with lofty disdain. J. R. Harris does introduce a pointless wet-fly dressing in his appendix to his book on entomology for anglers, but since Daddies are terrestial creatures, the sunk-fly approach is without value. Even so, this spurning of the Daddy is difficult to fathom, for where his race is prolific, he will serve the lake-fisher as faithfully as the Mayfly will serve the stream addict.

The life-cycle of the Crane Fly, which is the drawing-room name for the Daddy, is not so well known as that of the moth. Gardeners are well acquainted with them, for they hatch out from that border scourge, the Leather-jackets. Besides the common Crane Fly, the angler is likely to run into his bigger brother, the Marsh Crane Fly. The differences between different species are too insignificant to worry the angler.

The female fly lays its eggs in damp soil, usually about two or three hundred at a time, which develop into baby leather-jackets in a fortnight or so. Feeding on vegetable matter in the subsoil until the following summer, they then pupate, emerging as mature Daddies to start the whole process all over again.

The females can be spotted when they lay their eggs by pushing their pointed rear-ends into the ground. Lake-side fields provide the damp conditions they need, and then the weary spent-flies are blown onto the water in large numbers, where the trout are awaiting the banquet. The heaviest fall of these flies comes towards the end of the season, in late August and September, fitting in perfectly with the tapering off of the sedge-fly hatches. It is noticeable that in dry summers, when the meadows become rock hard, even near to the water's edge, that the females are unable to deposit their eggs. This last season at Weirwood, where I depend on the Daddy to provide me with a supper, the Daddy was virtually non-existent.

In Ireland, the value of the Daddy is so well appreciated that the boat anglers dap with the natural fly on the great loughs, using very long rods and light lines of floss silk. On our lakes, this practice would contravene the rules, and the artificial fly is but rarely used. I proved to my own satisfaction that this is a mistaken attitude, for the first time my prototype was tested on a dour day at Weirwood, it started rising fish. They were chasing the fly right up to the boat and slashing at it along-side. Unhappily, I had only constructed the one model by way of experiment, which soon disintegrated under this hammering.

The problem of designing an adequate artificial was not difficult. The pattern I eventually settled on was made by tying a detached Mayfly-body of plastic to a No. 12 hook. The wings are either hackle points, tied "spent", and any blue-dun, grey or light ginger colour will serve, with a red cock's hackle wound in front. Before the hackle is tied in, it is necesary to attach four legs. It is true that the natural fly possesses six, but to reproduce these would make a cumbersome fly. The material employed is either Pheasant Tail Cock fibres, each knotted in the middle, or nylon or bristle dyed black. I have also used the celluloid wings that Americans love to adorn their Dragon-flies.

It is easy to fish this artificial Daddy from a boat. The aim is to make the fly skip from wave to wave, using a very long leader and rod. In light airs, I attach a "butterfly" of tissue-paper about a yard above the fly, to catch the wind and carry the fly away from the boat. No one need fear that the fly is useless for bank fishing. Trout often penetrate the shallows close inshore if they notice numbers of exhausted flies being carried onto the water.

Trout take the Daddy in a different way to other flies. They often try to drown or swamp it first by big swirls and tail-smashes. It is vital to ensure that the fly has been securely taken before striking, and, even then, the strike must be delayed, since a trout appears to hold it lightly in his lips before swallowing it under water. Before I allowed for this, my usual immediate-reaction strike failed to hook several good trout.

"Personally I have never found it of much account as an angler's fly." Thus Courtney Williams dismissed another of my favourites, the Hawthorne Fly. This is strange, for he gives an effective copy of it. I am no critic of this respected authority, but it does seem that expert stream fishermen mistakenly apply their experiences to still water. Consider, a few terrestial insects are falling into the river. The current bears them away, perhaps to the safety of a piece of floating debris or a weed-bed where they may climb to safety. The same fly tumbling onto the surface of the lake is in a far more hazardous situation. There is but little drift to carry him. His struggles make a commotion which eventually attracts the attention of cruising fish. In fact, if you follow the fortunes of any large fly trapped in the surface film, you will rarely see it make its escape, but you will probably witness its downfall to a trout.

The Hawthorne Fly is classed by the angler as a Black Gnat, together with other insects of similar appearance, including Heather Fly, the House Fly and a darkish fly which swarms over the water at certain times, and which resembles the ordinary House-fly closely. But, of all these, the Hawthorne Fly has attracted most attention when I have been fishing. One day, when I was drifting along the shore of Denny's Island at Chew, there was such a fall from the trees that a heavy, preoccupied rise took place, and the artificial was eagerly accepted to the exclusion of other flies.

The appearance of the Hawthorne Fly is confined to the period during which the tree of the same name is in blossom, and it is recognisable by its size of about half-an-inch in length, its jet-black colour, and its long, hairy legs trailing behind it in flight. Nevertheless, it is advisable to carry a Black Gnat imitation throughout the season, for the similar Heather Fly is more common in August, while miscellaneous black flies may flutter across the surface to excite the trout at any time.

The boat fisherman may tie in a Black Palmer as a bob-fly to be dibbled on the surface, but for the accurate approach to the preoccupied rise, I am giving my favourite pattern, as listed by Courtney Williams:

Body—Black Ostrich Herl.
Wings—Pale starling.
Hackle—Black Cock.

I prefer to dress this on size 10 and 12 hooks, and I qualify this formula by the addition of a fine silver ribbing.

The list of dry-fly alternatives is by no means exhausted, but their application is limited, and would rather be termed as "minor tactics" than of general consideration. For instance, the Alder Fly is undoubtedly popular, but I have rarely encountered it in sufficient numbers to warrant the use of a fly more specialised than my dark sedge pattern. The Cow-dung depends on the animals that chase you along the banks. Water Board authorities prefer sheep.

For many years I have carried some artificial red and black ants, which are easily dressed by forming the distinguishable body shape with tying thread of the correct colour, then attaching white hackle-point wings sloping backwards, and finally the hackle to match the body-colour. Unfortunately, I have not yet witnessed one of those vast migrations of flying ants during my sojourns at the lake.

It is fun to experiment with these artificials at the vice. I made some excellent Bluebottles from balloon rubber, but they did not interest the fish. My huge floating dragon-fly makes an interesting study in sailing technique, but so far its score is nil. As in all tactics, it is necessary to lay down a dividing line between what is practicable and the fruitless exercise of imagination without basis. I have a good armoury; more armour would merely weigh me down.

CHAPTER X

THE SUNK LINE

WRITING THIS book has compelled me to list my tactics under certain headings. It has also caused some self-examination. What do I mean by tactics? Is it not sufficient to ascertain that, say, the Worm Fly is often killing at Chew? Why should I not fall into the customary practice of describing the effectiveness of various flies at different times and places? This would be approaching the trout by way of random fly-selection and method of working it. No doubt many anglers catch fish this way, for the local favourites provide the handiest method of coming to grips with a strange water on a quick visit.

This is not my understanding of tactics. My trout fishing is based on an appreciation of the quarry's behaviour in his environment. It means a study of the natural history of the fish, of entomology, and of the physical facts of the lake, its temperature changes, and its movement in wind. This does not lead to the confusion of scientific terminology, for there exist many works specially written to make these facts intelligible to anglers. These books I have listed separately.

But why start with the books? The angler has the advantage of being able to use the fishery as his own laboratory. He is able to refer his own observations back to the text-books, and, from my own experience, it widens tremendously the field of enjoyment. The image of the "bone-headed athlete", plunging straight into the water and casting automatically to the maximum of his effort then fades into oblivion.

At the same time, the discovery of the wide range of creatures upon which the fish feeds has to be rationalised to an intelligible range of flies. The word "fly" itself means more than an insect imitation. It is any confection of fur and feather that is delivered by the skill of casting with orthodox trout rod and tapered line.

When we consider visible trout activity, the tactics are planned logically. In discussing minnow, sedge and buzzer I may even give the false impression of dogmatic statement in my desire to lay the foundation for a systematic attack. But when we think of trout feeding near the bottom, or in middle water, we enter the field of conjecture, for very frequently there will be no sign of trout feeding. Occasionally there may be a clue from nymphs breaking to the surface, or we may know that certain waters are rich in Shrimp or Water-Boatmen. But, more often than not, the water will be inscrutable. My process is reversed, and I have to start with the fly and work back to the trout. Yet, even guesses may be inspired by observation.

Under these cirumstances, the angler will have to sink his flies deeply for any chance of success. Today lines are made to sink at various speeds. Slow sinking lines are ideal for searching the middle water whilst medium-speed sinkers are suitable for most reservoirs where the depth is not too great. The high density lines and fast sinkers are used for fishing the really deep holes, though they do compel the fly to be fished quickly if there's any weed or debris on the bottom. In addition, we have sink-tip lines where the body of the line floats and perhaps ten feet at the tip are of a sinking material, the perfect way to lift a nymph from a shallow bottom towards the surface.

We can also tie flies with a loop of nylon looping from the tail, round the hook bend and point, to be tied in before the hackle at the point, the so-called "brush off" system. The choice of nylon diameter for these weed-guards should be strong enough to fend off any weed filaments, yet not so strong as to prevent hook penetration when the trout seizes the fly. I find a nylon of about 6 lb b.s. suits flies up to size 10, and a 12 lb, b.s. is better for larger flies and lures.

It is now quite possible to retrieve the sunken fly through dense weed beds, where fish feed, without fear of snagging up, and to use normal fly-hooks rather than the specially shaped weedless hooks which I fear to trust.

I now turn to some of the imitations of natural food of trout to be fished in deeper water. The first of these is the Corixa, or Water Boatman. Although the traditional dressing has a white silk body, I incline to the view of C. F. Walker that the best colour is a sort of light beige, for which he used the fur of the Opossum, but my preference is for the light brown fur on the outside of a hare's mask. My tying is as follows:

Tag—fine silver oval, two to three turns, then ribbed up over the body.
Back—a strip of fibres from the dark speckled hen quill, tied in at tail end, taken over the body to be tied in again at the head, separated into two sections with figure-of-eight turns of silk, to form the paddles on either side. The back and paddles to be varnished.
Body—brownish-white fur from hare's mask, spun on thickly to make a fat body.

The natural Corixa shoots to the surface occasionally to collect an air supply, which action can be copied by fishing the weighted artificial with a floating or sink-tip line.

A second killer is the Freshwater Shrimp, also fished deeply and slowly. My tying is:

Tag—over gold tinsel, then ribbed over body as for the Corixa.
Back—olive nylon raffia (raffine) over the body, then varnished.
Body—pale olive seal's fur mixed with light brown fur from the hare's mask.
Hackle—pale olive under shank, short.

The dressing of the Shrimp should be taken some way round the hook shank to give the curved body effect of the natural, which can also be enhanced by padding the top of the hook shank with wool or raffia before the body fur is wound. This imitation can be weighted with an underbody of fuse wire, built up to give the same curved effect.

Until recently, the only imitation of the Fresh Water Louse was that of C. F. Walker, but it is most finicky to tie. A simpler pattern would have a grey partridge hackle divided on either side at the tail end of the fly, followed by a body of hare's ear ribbed with silver tinsel. Prolific in some waters, this pattern kills many fish at Sundridge lake, fished close to the bottom, very slowly. It, too, can be weighted with fuse wire.

Another deep-water denizen is the black snail, of which trout are inordinately fond. The best dressing is probably that of Tom Ivens, the Black & Peacock Spider, ribbed with a thick nylon. Personally, I often add a strip of black raffine, varnished, over the back of this fly to give some shell-like appearance.

I move on to the leech. One of the advantages of being in close contact with a fishery of my own is that I build up a picture of trout food. Sundridge is one of the richest larders I know, perhaps the richest, due to the alkaline flow of the River Darent. Although we must beware of relating every artificial to trout food (some lures merely exact a predatory response), I feel sure the Black Lure in various forms appears leech-like to the fish. The joined tandem especially slims down in the water and adopts a sinuous motion on the retrieve. In this lake, and many others, the leech is present, and the black variety, known as the Horse Leech, is preyed upon by fish.

We must beware of the danger of cramming into our fly boxes dozens of different patterns. If an angler fishes a water regularly then he should build up a picture of the trout food on the bottom. It's common sense not to fish the Corixa where it is absent. There's no need to master the intricacies of entomology to identify basic food items from the stomachs of spooned-out trout. We have an ample source of books in angling language, complete with coloured plates. Most of us recognise our jam-jar memories of Water Boatman, Tadpole (another Black & Peacock victim), Leech, snail, and Bloodworm.

It follows from this that we can build up, too, an underwater strategy for favourite fisheries. On strange waters there is usually a key, even if tradition or local report has to be relied on. Fly-fishermen have known for decades of the success of the Corixa at Blagdon, while alkaline waters normally yield hard-shelled creatures such as the snail.

Now, if I had to fish at random in deep water on a reservoir unknown to me, then I might have to guess as follows. Most lakes have a population of sedges, which resemble each other. I have a general sedge pupa pattern, called the "Caddis Case". It is very simple, the body being of ostrich herl, brown, olive or green, with matching back of nylon raffia. At the eye, to copy the head and emerging legs from the case, I tie in a hackle of similar body colour, clip it short, then wind in a few strands of peacock herl to make a small head. I cannot be sure if the fish will take this for what I intend though I may try to convince my friends. It could equally well copy the Damsel Fly larva, or a host of other creatures. It might just provoke a random feeding response in a hungry fish.

It doesn't really matter, for we shall never know the intentions of the trout. The important thing is that it gives me an intelligible tactic. It compels me to fish in a useful way, in a promising place, as along a sunken shelf, or by deep weed beds.

Finally, I can always fall back on various minnow imitations, using the word "minnow" loosely to cover a host of small fish and fry. I believe that actual feeding on small fish by trout is less than we think. The average flashy lure does not imitate small fish, one of the huge fallacies in fly-fishing. Nevertheless, when in doubt, it does make sense to work a proper minnow imitation along flooded ditches or the edges of weed and reed beds.

This is the hardest time for the imitative fly-fisher, when boredom is never far away. The water cannot be read. Nothing moves on a calm surface. The very deadness pervades the mind. We may fall into the error of visualising the reservoir as full as those rich, small lakes of entomological delight, like Sundridge, Two Lakes or Damerham. They are not, and their fauna is less varied and sparser. Even so, trout must feed, and upon this elementary fact, imitative tactics are structured.

CHAPTER XI

DWARFS AND GIANTS

THE DWARFS are the Angler's Curse. Every fly-fisherman experiences the frustrating occasion when the trout are pre-occupied with a tiny day-fly to the exclusion of all other food. The ultimate frustration is when a large dry-fly is completely ignored by a fish picking off these minute specks of life on either side of it; hence the name which is based upon the fisherman's reaction. In the first place, the reservoir man is unlikely to carry any fly of that size in his box, let alone one that matches. Yes, the Angler's Curse is virtually a day-fly, the species being called Caenis. I have decided to treat it separately because of the importance it has to trout. They adore it. And I am sure that fishermen think of a rise to the "Curse" as a distinct phenomenon, one in which they have little share.

Apart from their size, these flies are instantly recognisable by their broad wings of white or buff colour. They also have three tail whisks which are usually much longer than the body. The trout take them with gentle sips, but so avid is their feeding that the sip-like rings will often overlap, the expanding ripples colliding with each other on the surface. The rise may be to either the floating dun or spinner, or to the nymph right in the surface film.

We are used to thinking in terms of either a sunk fly or a floater, but I must stress again the importance of this surface film in still-water fly-fishing. At the surface, the molecules are more strongly drawn together, forming this elastic skin which holds and traps food for the trout. We remember the party trick of the floating needle, which is virtually held in this film. More important to the angler is the experiment of forcing a piece of velvet through the skin. The velvet takes on a sheen of silver due to the air trapped between the fibres by this molecular skin. Many aquatic creatures collect their air supply in this way, and the fly-dresser copies the silvery appearance of the descending air-sac with tinsel or lurex.

A fly can be designed to settle down into this surface film. The Gold-ribbed Hare's Ear is a fine example. Yet, it takes experience to fish the artificial in that position, as well as keen eyesight. With practice it can be achieved.

Another problem is recognising the difference in rise-forms of trout feeding on insects at levels in the water that are the merest fraction of an inch apart. Experience leads to the identification of the rather splashy rise to the fly floating on long legs above the water's skin, the gentler sip of the trout collecting food in the film itself, and the "humping" backs of fish mopping up nymphs just below the surface. Fortunately, these clues may be accompanied by the appearance of the insect itself. It is unwise to underestimate either the importance of the invisible wall, or its strength. I have illustrated how even a large moth is unable to break free.

I have discovered with Caenis imitations that trout accept them more readily when they settle down into the surface film.

Is it worth troubling over the rise to the "Curse"? I have cited one time when I was fortunate enough to take trout with consecutive casts. The other occasion was during an early morning hatch of Caenis at Weirwood, in the first years when the average weight of trout was high. The sun had not yet risen, when I spotted a sporadic hatch of Caenis in the quiet water beyond a weedy margin. The sipping rises gently troubled the stillness, and I made my first cast with the dry-fly to hook a heavy trout that rose instantaneously. He ran deeply into the body of the lake so that I was able to wear him down without disturbing the feeding ground. After a short time, I beached him successfully, and rapped his head on the heel of my wader. Leaving this trout shining in the pearly light of the time between dawn and sunrise, I primped up the hackles to repeat the cast towards the dimples that were still showing. I rose and hooked an identical brownie. I like to think that these were the only two fish working those hatching Caenis. Even as I unhooked the second trout, an evil chilly wind whistled up from the East, and it was a day of the sunk fly.

These fish fell victim to my favourite artificial for the Angler's Curse, a fly called the Grey Duster. The fly once brought me the limit of trout allowed at Weirwood before 10 o'clock in the morning, when there was a healthy rise to Caenis on the edge of the ripple.

The bodies of most Caenis are pale yellow or cream, in both Duns and Spinners, so it is scarcely worth the effort of concocting separate artificials. It is hard to lay down a definite body colour, for it varies from species to species, from lake to lake. The pelt of the rabbit from which the body-dubbing of the Grey Duster is taken, will furnish a wide range of choice. The fur next to the skin is blue, then progressing through grey to fawn. There are also some patches of white. The hackle is Badger Cock, white fibres with a distinctive black list to indicate the thorax. The tail whisks should be quite long, twice that of the hook shank, and cut from a spade Badger hackle. This makes the Grey Duster.

I have made reference to the importance of using first-class hooks. This is even more urgent when dressing minute flies for lake dry-fly. I have frequently lost trout on the hook being straightened out. Once I established a museum of these failures, and some half-dozen were of these Grey Dusters. I even had a formidable No. 8 Peter Ross wrenched into the near-horizontal by a smash take as I was lifting the line in order to re-cast. These Caenis must be made up on sizes 16 and 18. Since I fish a team of two, I design the point-fly as a fully-hatched Dun, standing erect on the surface, which is achieved by giving the fly five full turns of hackle as well as a bulkier tail. The dropper simulates the hatching nymph in the surface film. This seems to be the more killing technique, but the fly is simply a more sparsely hackled version of the dry-fly. This thinner dressing allows it to "settle down".

I put my faith in wide-gape hooks for these tiny flies. The ones which were most consistently reliable were Hardy's Payne hooks, but I have not been able to procure these for some time. Naturally, the small eyes mean fine points to the leader, perhaps even of only 2 lbs breaking strain. There are exceptions to every rule, and my hard-striking advice would only lead to lost fish if applied to the Caenis tactics. At the time when I felt that the "Curse" would rise at every Summer's dawn at Weirwood, it was my practice to put up a light dry-fly rod and stalk the individual trout. It is sporting fishing, for the scales are balanced from fly to leader, from leader to line, from line to rod. The casts were rarely more than 15 yards, and the hooks sent home by the traditional turn of the wrist. I have not seen those fabulous conditions since three years ago, and I feel they never may return.

It is only fair to add that other patterns have been recommended for dealing with the "Angler's Curse". Lunn's Yellow Boy, and a very small Coachman are firm favourites. More important is the preparation of leader and fly for this not uncommon eventuality.

My giant is something of an ogre, for it is nothing less than the Dragon Fly, the larva of which is the underwater tyrant. Its greed is such that it will seize and overcome even small fish of many times its own size.

Although C. F. Walker cites cases of trout being found stuffed full of the adult flies, I share his view that the fish probably only catch the females while they are egg-laying. It is the vulnerable nymph that again most frequently falls victim to the trout, for their size is such as to justify the rule of the biggest return for the least investment. Blagdon and Eye Brook are both lakes in which the trout appreciate the huge nymphs. At Blagdon, we have found them in stomach contents of trout, though the smaller cousin of the Dragon Fly, known as the Damsel Fly, was present in larger quantities.

Fly-dressers have been reluctant to invent artificials that necessitated the use of hooks of salmon size, for these larvae are upwards of an inch long. It is true that big lures are unpleasant to cast on a trout rod, and the hook is too rank in point and barb to drive home with the lighter rods. To a great extent this difficulty has been superseded by the advent of the tube fly, although a friend of mine in Alabama, who specialises in preparing Bass Flies, pointed out to me that the body of a fly may be extended beyond the length of the hook shank.

I am inclined to try a Damsel Fly nymph when I see many of the adult flies hovering over the water and along the margins. There seem to be two principal colours, a dull olive and a bright blue. I dress these on tubes of about an inch long, using seal's fur in the former case, and blue lurex ribbed with black wool in the second. I wind in a turn or two of matching hackle at the shoulder, and finish off with a large head of peacock herl. The blue nymph has a hackle of dyed Guinea Fowl, but in either case, a few fibres of Buck-tail would be an effective substitute.

An excellent scheme for switching the sizes of these nymphs, or indeed of all tube flies, is by dressing additional body sections on shorter tubes, which can be added to the leader or taken away as required. It is also a speedy way of varying the colour combinations of the tube equivalents of "terrors".

This special section devoted to these monstrous nymphs has been added because I have found them to be extraordinarily effective when fished near to the bottom. If the fly is wire-loaded, and given a minute or two to sink right down to the mud, when it is lifted sharply, a small smoke-screen drifts away from that place. The nymphs find stems of plants to crawl up to the surface, and one would be tempted to believe that this would be the ideal site for operations. In fact, I have killed some trout using the fly as a fast, mid-water pattern.

It is difficult to list the Damsel Fly in order of tactical importance. It is certainly not a pattern that I rely on, even though it kills fish on some waters. I recommend the carrying of two or three artificials to try on quiet days when fair numbers of the mature adults are in evidence, or if the first trout opened contains one or two of the larvae. Often I have mounted one as a "long-shot" and then I have been pleasantly surprised. This accounts for its separate treatment here.

CHAPTER XII

BLAGDON AND WEIRWOOD LAKES

THIS HAS been in the nature of a text-book, outlining tactical suggestions to help you catch more trout in the great reservoirs. When planning the work, I intended to include descriptions of two of our typical fisheries. It would have been easy to treat this in a similar way, by the presentation of technical data of the waters I chose. At the same time, this would have been a repetition of the information contained in the excellent booklets issued by the various water-board authorities that are responsible for the administration of the fisheries. The Bristol authority produces annually a fully-detailed breakdown of catches, maps of the lakes, and lists of regulations, all together in a finely illustrated publication. It is sent freely on request.

I promised myself a holiday in this chapter. Instead of repeating these facts, I decided to describe two waters which I know well, but which are entirely different in character. I wish to try to capture something of the atmosphere, and the way to do this is by telling of my experiences and impressions of them. One of these lakes has been long established. This is Blagdon, in Somerset. The other is a comparatively new reservoir in North-West Sussex. Although these fisheries are unalike, they represent the two poles between which most trouting will fall.

I imagine that three out of every four anglers heading for the Bristol lakes will be drawn to Chew. The fish are bigger, the area vaster. I must confess that I have no complaint against Blagdon's grand sister, for I have had some memorable days there. The very air is redolent of success.

To me, Chew has a touch of the "Affluent Society" fishified. The Lodge is designed in the modern idiom, and the gleaming Jaguar blends in well to these surroundings. I always expect to find the battered family saloon outside the weathered and mature Angler's Hut at Blagdon. It is a question of atmosphere, for here I feel no stranger. As soon as I step into the hut, seeing afresh the glass-cases with the mummified monsters of earlier years, or turning the pages of the ancient record books inscribed in the impeccable copper-plate handwriting of our grandfathers, I feel as if I have returned home.

In my opinion, Chew is reaching the peak of its perfection. There are days when even the novice angler will stagger drunkenly up to the Woodford Lodge heavily laden with a scarlet-spotted and rainbow harvest. This happens for the first few years of any rich and newly-flooded valley. After this, the fishing levels off as the food-supply from the meadows is consumed. From then on, only those who recognise the capricious whims of the lake and plan their tactics accordingly will enjoy consistent success. Eventually the golden days of Chew will be a memory—"You should have been here back in '65!" At last, even this will be said no longer, as the pile of record books grows higher and higher in the lounge.

So it was with Blagdon. The happy era is meticulously written in the books of the Music Hall days before the First World War. The stuffed monsters entombed along the walls bear silent witness, and you may find there the yellowing photograph of an Edwardian fishing party. The horizon of stove-pipe hats above mutton-chop whiskers drew my gaze, even while I was admiring the mammoth rods and nets clutched in their fists. Nowadays, Blagdon trout are a settled community, rewarding those who are faithful, but often spurning the casual visitor.

The lake lies between two escarpments, the Mendips and the Blackdown Hills. Occasionally I read disagreeable strictures in the angling press against poetic descriptions of lakes and rivers. I would defy the most detached, icy-blooded technician to fish a summer's day at Blagdon, and reduce it to a soulless formula of line weight and rod-taper. Any younger fisherman that had been brought up on a reading diet of Bernard Venables would remember his description "Failure at Blagdon" from his book *A Fisherman's Testament.* He recounts how he fished from a Thursday to the following Monday without touching a trout. But it was one short sentence that fired my imagination. "I knew I would return." This is the magic of Blagdon.

What a temptation to try to follow in the footsteps of a boyhood hero! I open again to my favourite passages. But what desecration to rehash the images of "smiling meadows". Bernard Venables described Blagdon in a way that makes further words superfluous. I need only reiterate that he caught no fish, but wrote "I knew I would return". But when I have nightmares, it is of a caravan-breeding scheme, runaway holiday camp or rampaging bungalow development swarming down the hillsides into the valley.

The high slopes prevent the early morning sun from slanting gently on to the water. One of the strange results is that you can be bitterly cold at one moment of a midsummer's dawn, and steaming hot the next. I have been compelled to quit the water to work blood into my stiffening fingers in early July hours, while a few minutes later, I have been stripping down to my shirt. The hills often protect the lake from the winds. Blagdon fishermen are used to contending with those deathly, bright calms that suddenly fall across the water.

Of course, the submerged features that once guided anglers, such as hedges and ditches, have long since blurred. When Bernard Venables first fished there, the local experts were able to point out these places. The old watercourse of the infant stream that was blocked to create the reservoir still influences the trout. This makes Rugmore point a popular rendezvous, for there, though wading through the shallows, the flies can be worked across the hidden channel.

The profounder depth of any natural reservoir lies near to the dam, and Blagdon is no exception. The most distant reaches from the dam are quite shallow. One large tongue of water biting into the land from the body of the lake is Butcombe Bay, where deeps can be reached from comparatively short casts from the bank. The waist of the lake forms a happy medium, positions like Orchard Bay and Rainbow Point combining the best of both worlds.

The trout take the fly eagerly, though above all it is a "minnow water". The dawn reconnaissance will certainly reveal one or two immense "sticklebackers", as huge as any of the fish in all of the Bristol lakes. These monsters are hard to cover, for they rush into the shallows with gaping mouths, scooping up their prey and whipping back into the depths, all in the twinkling of an eye. Lesser trout may be seen beating up the weed-beds, the frenzied arrows of the needle-like fry betraying their activity.

In the early Spring, the Chironomidae will become increasingly more important to the trout, and they will continue to hatch right through the Summer. A small number of these buzzers may scamper off the surface in the late morning, but the hatch should be in full swing by the late afternoon. The flies may be bursting from deepish water where the trout will be seen "bulging" as they mop up the vulnerable pupae suspended under the surface film. Later, the picture is confused, for the trout may also attack the adult flies returning to the water to lay their eggs.

The Blagdon sedge population seems more sparse than at neighbouring Chew, and the fish do not seem to relish the small dark sedges that appear in the forenoon. The ubiquitous Olives hatch in the rapidly warming shallows, though often their appearance is restricted to a limited area.

I am in danger of slipping back into the technical groove. Fly-fishing is more than the application of intelligence to trouty problems. Consciously, or unconsciously, we absorb the atmosphere of our surroundings. In a tranquil environment, we are at peace with ourselves. Perhaps these are the only occasions when tightly nerved people like myself really unwind. This is why I become so incensed when someone or something breaks the spell. Over the seasons the memories pile up, fragments of various days. Some of these are irritating, such as the hot Summer's day when the holiday-makers descended in force to picnic and play football on the grassy verges. Another time, a couple changed into swimming costumes and bathed in the lake, only to be chased semi-clothed through the woods by the bailiffs.

There was an occasion when a gang of poachers in a nearby field brought down a duck into the corner of the bay where I was hidden from sight behind a tree. One of them shinned over the fence and waded through the rushes to retrieve it, when he suddenly was out of his depth, and had to swim for dear life. I shouted, but the peculiar acoustics of the valley in the silent morning made my voice ring with a hundred echoes. The poachers, thinking themselves beset by gamekeepers, fled across the hill-side.

These are major incidents. There are other mere episodes that refuse to be thrown out of my mind. One is the image of a great white owl I scared out of a tree when I was tramping along the path in the half-light of early dawn. I still see him flapping lazily away until swallowed up in the mists rising from the meadows. And humorous memories never die. I was beginning to slip into the double-haul rhythm, which is, as yet, rarely seen on our reservoirs. I was contented with a distance of about 30 yards, fished out the cast, and started to lay back the rod for the next "shoot". As I turned my head to follow the unfolding line behind me, my eyes met those of a man who was gawping at me from the window of his car. My hand slipped on the nylon, and the result was a glorious birds' nest.

I have described elsewhere the capture of my biggest brownie from Blagdon, a fine specimen of 3 lbs 6 ozs. This would not be an exceptional size from Chew, but here the trout run smaller. One of the prejudices against the reservoir trout is the belief that their fighting powers are diminished through being artificially reared in a hatchery. The strange thing about this argument is that it is paraded by some anglers who sing the praises of carp that have also been reared in stock-ponds. In both cases, the fish are in their wild surroundings at an early age, and are acclimatised completely before they fall victim to rod and line. The only circumstances that I believe to ruin the sporting qualities of fish, apart from disease and parasite, are the continual catching and returning of specimens in over-fished waters. All sizeable trout are killed, and on some waters the rules insist on trout being killed, irrespective of size.

The simplest way of giving you an idea of Blagdon lake is to take you there on a day's fishing. We are staying in the "Live and Let Live Inn" which is one of those rare pubs run to the fisherman's timetable. Tomorrow is forecast as one of those typically warm, unclouded June days, so we tell Mr. Gulliver, the landlord, that we shall be up before the lark and back before breakfast with a couple of trout. Then we go to bed early, having set the alarm.

It is dark when we wake up. Soon we have stealthily crept forth with our tackle to walk down the lane to the lake. The false dawn has given way to the genuine article, and the promise of the sun is glowing rosily along the ridge of hills. A ghostly mist is drifting across the fields, stinging our fingers and cheeks. From Blagdon village behind us, a cockerel shouts "Good Morning" to be answered by another from Butcombe across the lake. At the foot of the hill, we follow the sign of the fish to the hut to collect our licences from the automatic dispenser. Then we follow the path along the margin of the lake.

I am keeping well away from the water's edge, for I am looking for signs of trout harrowing the fry in the shallows. Now and again there is a dimpling rise to microscopic midges, but these are casual wanderers which would be difficult to intercept. Then I find what I am seeking. The fringes of a long weed-bed lift themselves up in a boiling commotion. A fish is flushing out the minnows, forcing them up to the surface. There is, as yet, no direct sunlight, so the Green and Brown tube fly is a better choice than a Jersey Herd or Alexandra. The surface of the lake being so untroubled, we slip our tubes on to knotless tapered leaders of 12 yards.

We will fish this one together, slipping stealthily into the water some 20 yards above the place where the trout is still furiously thrashing the weeds. Now we are parallel to the limits of the weed-bed, working out the shooting heads into the air. You will make the first cast to drop the fly beyond the disturbed water, drawing the fly close along the edge of the green blanket. If you catch up on weed, free it gently, or lay your rod over to clear the line for my attempt. One lay back and haul, forward cast, haul, and shoot, and the fly is right on target, with the shooting head floating well and the nylon extended. The fly is now being stripped in jerkily. There comes the great swirl, and you lean back hard on the rod. He is on! Then you are exerting side strain to lever him into the open water. Soon I will net your first Blagdon brownie. There he is, a fish of 2 lbs.

Now we will move on to Rainbow Point, still prospecting for trout before the banks are lined with other anglers. The weeds here are sparser, and there are swarms of sticklebacks in red mating-finery. The sun has just climbed over the low hills, dispersing the wraithes of mist. Was that a slight rocking of the weeds? I will work a Jersey Herd along the margins to find out. This fly is taken deeper, with no surface swirl, only a fierce tug and the line streaking away. That makes two trout for breakfast, so we return.

We will come down to the lake later on in the day. What a difference meets our gaze. Cars are parked on the grass verges, and the banks are lined with a rank of fishermen at intervals, each one casting and retrieving mechanically. We are travelling light, with dry-fly rods of 9 feet in length, one bag with a fly-box, and some spare leaders. It would be pointless to elbow in between two settled anglers, so let us stroll down to the unpopulated shallows at the far end of the lake.

There we sit down on the grass to study the situation. The sun is high above us, the water appears to be lifeless.

There is an almost imperceptible dimpling of the surface some twelve yards out. Then we discover a few Olives struggling from their nymphal cases, before skittering away towards the rushes. Was one of those dimples slightly stronger than the rest? Surely it was! There might be a fish leisurely intercepting the nymphs on their way to the surface.

I will try to catch this one, and a "wet" Greenwell is quickly tied to the end of the leader, and moistened thoroughly between the fingers to achieve a good entry. The distance is not very great, so I make a cast from a kneeling position by the water's edge. The fly cuts through the surface film beyond the dimpled area, while I begin to recover it very slowly indeed. Then comes the kidney-shaped whorl towards the point where the last foot of nylon dips below the surface. I strike with a full-blooded swing of the rod, scrambling to my feet at the same time. Immediately I know that this is a heavier, more doughty opponent.

"He's on! Net!"

I am coming further up the bank to control this fish. He has already been turned from sanctuary in the weed-beds and is bolting for the open water. I feel the splice slip between my fingers as I slow down the sizzling line. This is the orthodox double-taper floating line that I use with my dry-fly rod for prospecting along the banks on hot summer days, so I realise that more than 30 yards of this heavy material is threatening to drag free the hook unless I can quickly recover it on to the drum. This is when the full power of the rod must be bent against the fish. He has halted his dash and is beginning to move parallel to the shore. Still keeping deep, he must be a brownie.

"Get down to the edge, and keep low. I'll try to bring him over the net this time!"

I start to "horse" him in. First the splice returns home, then the line feels thicker between my fingers as the belly is recovered. A bit more "stick" and he is moving towards the net. One smart swoop with the net. A 3-lb brownie is an excellent fish for Blagdon!

Now it is time for an afternoon snooze under this tree in the cool shade, and in the late afternoon we will cross to the other side of the lake in anticipation of a hatch of buzzer from the deeper water in Butcombe Bay. This depth of several feet is easily gained from the bank, so there is little need to change to the long-casting, shooting-head routine.

As we arrive, keeping a respectful distance from the water, I point out a tree by the margin of the lake. This will make an excellent forward observation post to watch along the line of the shore. Here, the weeds grow to but a few feet from the bank, and then the floor of the lake shelves steeply away into black water. The buzzers, hatching from the deep water beyond, regard these weeds as their first landfall. Sure enough, there are a few weaving in towards them.

"Did you see that?"

There it was again, the speckled tail fin of a rainbow trout breaking the water close by the weeds. It is now your turn. One buzzer nymph is all that you need on this tranquil surface, but grease the nylon to the last 6 inches. I have noticed that these earliest buzzers are black. The "Footballer" is an effective, all-round pattern.

This is delicate work, this stalking of individual fish that are working near to the bank. If you were to plunge into the waters in your waders, you would drive them into deeper water, and then you needs must fall into the mechanical distance casting in the hope that the law of averages would come down on your side. A feeding trout is one that can be caught, providing that the essential rules of concealment are followed. On very still surfaces, few anglers can cast beyond the limits of the disturbance that they create. The greater the effort, transferring the weight from one foot to the other, the wider will spread the ripples.

Fortunately, you know your tactics, and make the false casts from behind the barrier of rushes. The correct distance is gauged in the air, and the fly drops neatly into the target area.

"Strike!" That tailing rise means he is moving down to take the sinking nymph. You lay the rod over to lever the trout away from the feeding zone in case there are others dining in his company. The rod is kept low to prevent him from floundering on the surface. You play him to your right, but he is only a pound or so. Now you must try for another. Yes! Another rainbow of identical size.

"Did you notice those small dark sedge-flies?"

The trout here are not fond of them, but there may be a heavy evening rise tonight. There often is after these sultry days. We will switch to the shooting-heads now, and mount a team of buzzers of mixed colours, black, red, and green. When the rise reaches its climax, it will be impossible to single out individual fish. It is far better to comb a wide area.

As the sun slips down towards the hills, we continue to cast rhythmically, retrieving the buzzer nymphs through the period of the evening rise. When it reached its climax, the water was literally boiling. And now the dusk is beginning to fill the valley. The lights of Blagdon village are twinkling high above us, yet we have only caught one further fish each. This is often a time of bitter disappointment and frustration. It seems, at first, as if each cast must surely produce a trout, but as the evening wears on, despair replaces hope. The flies are right, the time is right, but the water is so filled with food that the artificials might well be missed. I much prefer to rely on the local hatches that I discover during my daytime wandering, though this cuts right across the accepted tenets of fly-fishing.

It is almost dark, but as we stroll back to the lane, I will unwind the stout cast with my moth imitation and have one last cast from under the pine trees. I make a short, high cast, allowing the fly to land with a hefty plop. As I begin to work it in jerks across the water, a fast-moving furrow overtakes the moth's wake, and they meet in a great turmoil of water. I strike hard. For an instant, I am connected to the hugest fish of the expedition, then suddenly the line is slack. It is time to pick up the bags.

I have compressed into one day the tactics that might be applied over a number of trips, according to the fly on the water, the minnows in it and the observed behaviour of the trout. There have been days when a rapid change of tactics has been matched to conditions to return a fine haul of trout. Last Whitsun was one such occasion, when I took an early-morning sticklebacker on a Green and Brown. As soon as the sun was bright on the water, I caught another on a Jersey Herd tube-fly. In the late afternoon, two rainbows fell to buzzer nymph, just as described in the imaginary visit. Finally, the evening rise, though prolific, was fruitless, but a further fish succumbed to the last cast of a Hoolet.

Blagdon is a mellow lake.

Entirely different to Blagdon is the character of Weirwood, though it must be considered as more typical of the run-of-the-mill trout reservoirs up and down the country. In the South-east, we have always been poorly served for trout fishing, particularly with the artificial fly. It is true that I served my apprenticeship on one of the tangled Wealden streams, but, when young, I was part mountain-goat. Generally, those of our streams that do hold a meagre stock of trout, the Kentish Teise or the Sussex Ouse, lend themselves more readily to the wiles of the spinner and drop-minnow expert rather than the fly-fisherman. It is true that the Hastings fly-fishers have two lakes near Battle, Darwell and Seddlescombe, the latter containing a small number of very big brown trout. When Weirwood opened, it seemed as if our troubles were over.

We tend to forget that the primary function of these reservoirs is to supply water for domestic and industrial consumption. In the case of Weirwood, it was constructed for the Crawley New Town, one of our post-war satellites of London. We have not yet reached that stage of social development when fisheries are created purely for recreation, as in other countries. The fishery is but a sideline of the Water Board. It is impossible for the Fisheries Officer to control all of the physical factors of his fishery. He cannot drain his lake, plough up the bottom, quick-lime it and flood it again. He cannot fertilise his water with phosphates, increase the alkalinity with lime, or poison the coarse fish with rotenone. Once coarse fish gain entry into these lakes, they breed. The introduced trout spawn with difficulty, and it is improbable that the rainbows spawn at all naturally. The brownies seem able to shed their spawn, particularly if a leat enters the lake over a bed of gravel. Certainly, we have caught fingerling brownies at Weirwood, but rainbows never. These sad circumstances would be mitigated if the authorities had their own hatcheries where ripe fish, trapped in the reservoir, could be stripped of ova and milt, and the fertilised eggs reared artificially. Alas, many fisheries buy their stocks at current prices from established fish-farms, and so have the worst of both worlds. How long will the rainbows last before dying of being spawn-bound? I think it averages at about two years after stocking, three at most.

This is the background to Weirwood. As is natural with newly-flooded land, the first open year was staggeringly successful. It was not long before the coarse fish made themselves known. Earlier, rudd were a thorough pest, but enthusiastic netting has brought them under control. Now, as in many of these lakes, the perch is the chief culprit, both in competition for food as well as the artificial fly. Worse is to follow, for in one rainy period, a lake higher up the infant Medway burst its banks and a consignment of carp was carried down into the congenial surroundings of Weirwood. Last season, a companion fishing a corixa on the bottom, was fortunate enough to hook a respectable bream. How long will it be before the pike arrive?

During this period, the average weight of trout has declined, even though the yearly catch is maintained at a figure of over three thousand. The fact that the lake affords trout fishing still is mainly due to the enthusiasm and hard work of its staff, and the Chief Bailiff, Ken Sinfoil.

The Bristol lakes are in the fortunate position of having both a rich food supply and their own hatchery. Chew can almost afford an incursion of coarse fish; in fact, their fry supplement the trouts' diet. In poorer waters, the trout suffer, as well as the angler who curses for paying to catch undersized, suicidal perch. In spite of the continuous netting at Weirwood, the perch problem is as severe as ever, I myself, having hooked them in threes. In this country, we are not sufficiently concerned with our environment to make lakes for one purpose only, trout fishing. We try to fit it in as a by-product of an industrial process. Without a lucky combination of circumstances, it will not work, for the simple fact is that Man has to be able to control all of the physical factors of the fishery, especially the numbers of fish and their relationship to the food supply. It would mean all of the factors I have mentioned, periodic draining, leaving fallow, reflooding and adjustment of the alkalinity of the water, correct stocking from hatcheries, and fertilisation. The bald truth is that we care so little for our environment that we refuse the expense and the trouble. Our fishing would cost more.

All we can hope to achieve at present is a more progressive tinkering with these problems. For example, there is little point in netting last year's hatch of perch, if this season's jellied progeny is allowed to become fry. The perch come into the shallows to spawn in the early spring, and the eggs are so prolific that the basket-nets are festooned with them. Why not resort to "faggoting"? This is the placing of bundles of twigs in the margins, which, when covered in the spawn, are removed and the eggs destroyed.

In the close-season for coarse fishing, local Clubs should be invited to assist with the netting programme on the understanding that they are allowed to keep the coarse fish they remove for their own waters. At Weirwood, this would be bound to include a number of healthy carp. My own Club at

Haywards Heath had its entire stock of carp decimated in the Wobblegate water during the infamous winter of recent memory. Such Clubs would be glad of the opportunity in view of the high cost of replenishment. I have always been offended by the rule to kill all coarse fish caught during a fishing expedition to a reservoir, and I wish the authorities would provide net-enclosures for every mile of bank so that anglers who wished to do so, could keep their fish alive to put into the pool.

I am also dubious of the wisdom of stocking heavily with rainbows in preference to the native brown species. The latter can at least reproduce himself to a certain extent in most reservoirs. Even the fact of being able to empty the roe ensures a longer life than the spawn-bound rainbow. The possibility of an over-wintering stock gives a number of larger fish to start the following season, and better chance for the specimen hunting fly-fisherman of an eventual whopper. I have a shrewd suspicion that the brownie is more efficient as a pruner of coarse-fish stocks, which is why I have tried to bring into truer perspective the minnow-insect relationship to the reservoir trout.

As to Weirwood itself, it is a vast lake of some 250 acres, formed by erecting a dam across the infant Medway near Forest Row. Although it lacks the spectacular scenery of Blagdon, it does have the gentle, rural charm of Sussex. Low, green hills roll away into the distance, pierced here and there by an ancient spire. At one point, those curious, sandy rocks that bring a wild-west atmosphere to parts of the Weald are clearly visible from the bank. Two memories I have of Weirwood. One is the smell, a tangy, marshy sensation that tingles in the nose. And nowhere have I heard so many skylarks. They climb and sing the live-long day.

Unlike Blagdon, many of the features of the flooded land are traceable. Here and there, a ditch plunges beneath the water; a treacherous place for wading, this, but before the invasion of the perch, it was a fine strategy to work a minnow-type fly along the gully. When the waterline recedes in high summer, the stumps of once-mighty oaks and remains of crumbling farm-buildings are resurrected.

I imagine the soil to be acid. For years I assiduously fished the river that is to become the Medway. At Hartfield, merely a mile or two below Weirwood, it is a clear, gurgling brook flowing between cows and buttercups. It is a delightful stream to fish, though the trout are lean and active. In Kent, a reservoir hollowed into the chalky subsoil of the foot of the Downs would grow trout as sturdy as those that once lived in the unpolluted Darenth at the turn of the century. You may still find crayfish there. Even though Weirwood appears to produce the occasional prolific hatch of Cinnamon Sedge and Silverhorn, I feel the dice are loaded against the trout. Always it comes down to the control of the physical factors of a fishery, the difference between Alex Behrend's Two Lakes, and the Southern and Midland reservoirs.

The day may dawn when we wake up to the practice of other countries. We may realise that environment and recreation in pleasant surroundings are as important to the well-being of man as his food, sleep and work. Then we will create trout fisheries (among others) for one purpose only, to provide fly-fishing. And then, too, we will apply the knowledge of the scientists who study fish culture. But until that day, we must rely on fisheries like Weirwood, being a combination of many purposes that prevents its exploitation as a trout fishery. In the meanwhile I am grateful for those facilities that do exist, and thankful that one or two enthusiastic fishery officers continue to perform an impossible task. This is the lesson of Weirwood.

CHAPTER XIII

TOWARDS A TACTICAL PHILOSOPHY

WE CAN never be sure why the trout takes the fly. We can only be sure why we want it to take the fly. We can never become entirely purist in still water fly-fishing because of the feeding behaviour of the fish. On chalk streams, Skues pondered the reasons for the "take", breaking it down into several categories, some based on hunger, curiosity, aggression, provocation and so forth. In lakes and reservoirs, we can be positive of two types of feeding, one at random, the other selective.

Random feeding behaviour is caused by sheer lack of food and is typical of early season, before sunlight is strong enough to warm the shallows thus releasing oxygen from the aquatic vegetation by photosynthesis, and insect life is dormant. Trout can suffer the pangs of hunger while hunting fruitlessly over sleeping larders, because they are programmed by nature to recognise their prey by its activity. At this time there is insufficient activity to impress a picture onto the primitive brain of the fish, so almost any movement, flash or vibration in the water excites the trigger-response. The lure, the traditional wet fly and the fry imitation are obviously indicated.

As the water temperature increases, everything changes, and as the inert winter-chemicals become unlocked in the depths, exploding the plankton food-chains into life, the deep lakes stratify into thermal layers and weed beds grow in the shallows. Insect populations become active, as do other fauna, and when one of these becomes prolific at a time and place in one of its active stages of life, then the trout becomes preoccupied with it to the exclusion of almost any other food form. This is when the correct imitation fished in the right behaviour pattern is essential and is what many river men call "true fly-fishing". On still water it produces the surface rises to nymph and larva, even on occasion to floating fly. It creates the urge to hunt down gathering shoals of fry around weed fronds. Unseen in the deeps there's the harrying of corixa, shrimp, fresh-water louse, sedge larvae, so that we wonder at the stomach of the fish crammed with creatures of the same colour and shape.

Preoccupied feeding cuts down our successes with lures as the season advances, and although those with limited imagination fish the flashers throughout the year, the intelligent tactician follows the cyclical development of the fishery, day by day, adapting his flies and fishing methods to what he sees on or near to the surface, or what he surmises is happening in the depths. Yet, fly-fishing is not entirely mechanical, for we do it for pleasure and, this being admitted, most fly-fishermen prefer to catch a trout by deceiving it when it is feeding with preoccupation, for it is the supreme test.

I've described how I offered the light shooting head alternative as against the old-style long, slow rod. Since those days we have discovered how to drive a fly-line by double haul with much lighter rods, so much so that this is probably the dominant trend in tackle for still water. Two other changelings were dropped into old-fashioned cradles by the first edition, the movement towards imitative flies when indicated, and the restatement of the case for the dry fly which was considered as practically useless during the fifties and sixties.

The nature of fisheries has changed, too, and although new reservoirs have been created, the development of leisure has surrendered much of our exclusive rights to other water-users. We lose areas to yachtsmen and banks are corralled off for day trippers. Fly-fishing at Chew cannot be as pleasant as it was before. It would be better for anglers and boatmen to use the lake on different days, as they do on some Cornish lakes.

We have seen, too, the expansion of the smaller, commercial lake fishery, pioneered at Two Lakes and Coldingham Loch, then followed by Packington and others. These lakes can be tucked away into urban areas, oases of tree-screened peace in the desert of chrome, glass and concrete. The fishing may have to be expensive, especially if the owner has to depend on it for his living, but they ease some of the pressure from the rod-crushed facilities at reservoirs. The smaller lake fishery enjoys almost total control over stocking, food supply, weed and coarse fish, and disease. The quality of the fish is almost always good, even though, in common with all modern trout fisheries, the put-and-take policy has to be applied.

While recusants like myself long for the wild trouting of yesteryear, the cold truth is that never before in our history have so many huge trout been taken on fly by all sorts and conditions of men. This must be good.

Another great change has been the increase in fly-fishing instruction, even if we seem unable to agree to accepted standards of qualifications for professional instructors. When the first edition was mooted, tuition was mainly in the hands of the professional teacher, giving individual lessons for fees but since then Local Authorities have started evening classes in fly-fishing and fly-tying. Tackle firms organise holiday courses, and even self-instruction has been made easier by volumes of advice in journal and book alike. Many may argue that the competent and incompetent instructor can both thrive on the great thirst for knowledge. Soon we must have a widely accepted body, respected by reputable instructors, and answerable to one of our National Organisations, like the National Anglers Council, or the Salmon & Trout Association. At present, anyone can describe himself as a Game-Fishing Instructor in an advertisement.

In 1966, though, it was easier to predict the future course of still water fly-fishing. The tackle trends were clear, the changes in casting technique would have to come. Today, it's harder to foresee change. In 1968, carbon fibre was to be the new fly-rod material, and when I questioned this, both for economic and technical reasons, I was told brusquely that the new carbon fibre fly-rod was on the point of arriving. Here, in 1973, it still hasn't come in prototype form, let alone to replace hollow glass.

Hollow glass seems assured for some years to come, for, given that line speed is the secret of distance casting, we can now build tapers in glass that are so fast that the line turnover is too fierce to control. Marginal improvements we have. Nylons for leaders, especially where fine points are required, can be one third less thick for the same breaking strain as regular nylons, so that brands like "Nylorfi" are being used more and more. Tungsten-carbide steel rod rings are proof against the faster moving line for the new casting techniques. Spigot ferrules of hollow glass eliminate the dead spots in the action of the rod where the old brass ferrule used to be, with its stress point on either side.

What of the fish itself? Promises of the Sunbeam trout and new Jumbo strains have fizzled out. We are stuck with our two old pals, the rainbow and the brownie. About the latter we know much, but next to nothing of the former since little scientific research has been carried out in Britain. Its short life span in still water, though thought to be associated with inability to spawn, is nevertheless a mystery. In smaller, deep lakes, stream fed, it winters through more happily than in the great, more static reservoirs with their extensive shallows, where their post-introduction span may not exceed the year's end. The rainbow is the basis for the "put and take policy".

This is the policy of a high turnover of fish, replacing them as they are caught, with new stock in penny packets. It allows intensive fishing, especially in small areas of water, and it is an economic necessity. Like it or not, our fisheries will be run on this basis from now on. If catches are largest on reservoirs in early season, the odds are that the bulk of trout taken each year are caught within weeks, even days of their introduction.

The greatest change in fly-fishing attitudes was caused by the opening of the vast Grafham reservoir in an area formerly dominated by coarse fishing interest. Many anglers who otherwise wouldn't have dreamed of taking up a fly-rod suddenly found a way of passing the close season, even those who previously had attacked reservoir fly-fishing became converts. The free-taking and hard fighting rainbows grew rapidly over the newly flooded land, and, until the food stocks were levelled off and competition from increasing numbers of coarse fish became a factor, Grafham certainly was the best trout fishery in Europe. It made both a demand and a financial reward to programme other new reservoirs for fly-fishing, while it boosted the development of specialised tackle for the growing market.

From 1970, I developed a small still water trout fishery of my own, at Sundridge, in Kent. This was a worked out gravel pit fed by the River Darent, a true chalk stream from the North Downs. Sundridge had established its reputation for large fish by its third year. Some of these were wild brown trout from the river, which had made their home in the lake, but the bulk were fish stocked at mixed weights and growing fast in the alkaline water. In the first year, one of the Sundridge members, Mr. Lyddon, landed a rainbow of 6 lb 11 ozs.[1] In the third year, over three thousand fish were recorded in the Club book, demonstrating the intensive crop to be taken from a fifteen acre lake.

Until this experiment, gravel and sand pits were thought to be poor homes for trout, and some earlier experiments had fizzled out, leading to a switch to coarse fish. Sundridge proved that these old workings can be used for fly-fishing if the correct policy is carried through. The first two years were dour, but the emphasis must be directed to building up fish population for the future, with strict bag limits. The stock must be introduced with a view to surviving the winter for future sport. The depth of gravel pits keeps average water temperatures low in summer, which trout like, but it is vital

[1] 'A rainbow of 8 lb 2 ozs was taken in 1973 by Ralph Johnson, of Canterbury.'

to establish shallower bays where sunlight can reach the bottom for food growth.

Our main problem was that trout liberated into alkaline water find rich feed on the bottom, with crustacea and the like. Only when the population has grown sufficiently to prune this stock of food will the trout come to the surface in response to hatches. Fishing continuously with sunk line and fly is boring. Since coarse fish never reproduce themselves prolifically in deep pits, the introduction of trout and the consequent fly-fishing policy may be quite painless.

The third year at Sundridge produced the first reliable surface rises and floating fly-lines, nymphs and dry flies began to figure largely in the returns.

It is to the tactical development of the fly-fisherman that this book is addressed. One other change in the man himself is welcome. More and more are accepting that fly-tying is as essential a part of the competent anglers' make-up as casting itself. With this goes a practical understanding of the natural history of lakes, including entomology. The growth of imitative fly-fishing is welcome, too, while I believe that C. F. Walker's book *Lake Flies and their Imitation* will prove to be a landmark. A cautionary note is that while Commander Walker's patterns were exercises in perfectionism, practical tyers will be wiser to strengthen and simplify them, without loss of effect.

An adaption is necessary when moving from the larger reservoir to the new, smaller lakes. When fishing at "Two Lakes", where I took a rod in 1968, I was struck by the way in which visitors from reservoirs often failed to adapt to small lake conditions, hurling their flies across the water while lining fish under their feet. Those who habitually fish both types of water realise that they need a different basic approach. On smaller lakes, the water close to you is very important. You must not alarm fish there. You use land to put distance between rod-tip and target. You may stalk fish from behind cover, as on a chalk stream. You may anchor the boat to fish an area, instead of the usual drift on big waters. You may even stalk fish by cautious boat manouevres, as I have done frequently.

Fish in small lakes are in closer contact with Man, his rod and line flash or shadow, his heavy footfall or his noisy paddle. Reservoirs seem to breed in many anglers the false feeling of safety in distance. The careless wader wallowing through the shallows thinks another fish will pass by later, when his bow-waves have subsided. Such commotion in a smaller lake would be disastrous as trout, though still cruising, also move into localised areas where food is abundant. To drive them out of it is folly.

Fly-fishing, like all sports involving some professionalism and commercial interests, has those human strands of competition, conflicting advice, sometimes of jealousy. It may be hard for the average angler to clear his thoughts in such a bemusing atmosphere. What is the test of an argument or theory? Does it make sense? Does it work? Those with rod in hand or fly in vice are not competing each with the other, for the only true critic is the trout. The greatest asset is adaptability to changing conditions, changing by the progress of the season, and also of each day. This tactical adaptation is based on sound casting technique, tackle within the limits of physique and experience, plus a sound basic knowledge of the fish in his environment.

Fly fishing isn't easy, but it has the virtue of being thoroughly enjoyable at every stage of its development.

APPENDIX I

CASTING SEQUEL

The diagrams of the casting sequel are based on the author's light shooting head system, using the double-haul technique. A modern tackle system would use a light, fibre glass rod with fastish action, such as the 8 ft 10 ins "Two Lakes" rod. The shooting head would be 33 feet cut from the end of a "Fast Taper" D.T. 8 line, joined by small loop to 40/100 nylon monofilament. Throughout the casting routines there should be a complete absence of strain.

Fig. 1. This shows the position of peak-power on the back cast, with full extension of the left-hand on the first haul. The feet are well spaced, to give good balance and allow weight transference onto the back foot. The caster has advanced his left foot so that his head can turn easily to watch the passage of the line to the rear.

Fig. 2. The power application has now finished on the back cast, and the rod is still flexing against the squeeze of the hand and thumb pressure on top of the handle. The still-flexing rod is drifting back behind the shoulder, line extending behind and the body weight is fully transferred onto the right foot.

Fig. 3. The line extends fully behind the caster, pulling on the left hand, which, from the position shown, feeds line back through the rings, bringing the left hand close to the lowest rod ring, preparatory to the second half. The left hand never releases line on the back cast.

Fig. 4. Peak power position on the forward cast, the rod driving forward, the left hand hauling line down from the lowest rod ring and the weight swinging back onto the left foot as the body and shoulders turn into the forward cast.

The line haul coincides with the forward punch of the rod, but in practical fishing, this haul must be sweet and free from vigorous jerks.

Fig. 5. The rod has reached the climax of the forward cast, where its movement is checked to allow the head to stream out over the water, when the shooting line is released by the left hand. The weight of the body is now fully on the front foot and the body and shoulders facing completely towards the direction of the cast.

The purpose of these diagrams is to give the effect of a continuous action. The failing of all photographs and drawings is that they tend to fill the mind with "frozen" postures which the novice strives to attain. The caster should remember the purpose of the cast, and not seek to reach isolated stages of it.

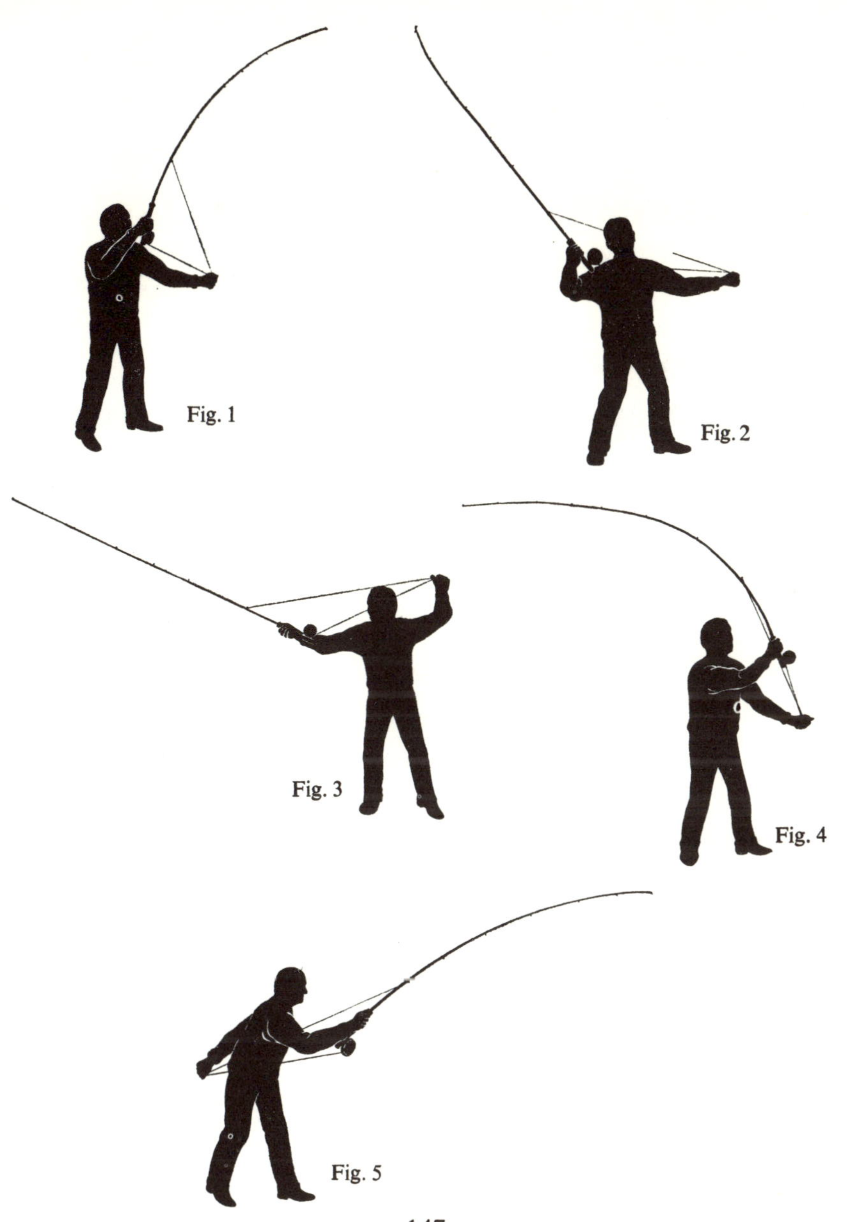
Fig. 1
Fig. 2
Fig. 3
Fig. 4
Fig. 5

APPENDIX II

DRESSINGS OF ARTIFICIAL FLIES USED BY THE AUTHOR

Minnow Tactics

Green & Brown Tube Fly

Body—Alternate turns of green and brown ostrich on a one inch tube, polythene for high water, metal covered for deep work.

Ribbing—narrow gold lurex.

Head—peacock herl.

Jersey Herd Tube Fly

Body—gold lurex, on tubes as above.

Hackle—hot orange goat's hair.

Head—peacock herl.

Peter Ross

Tail—tippet.

Body—silver lurex, ribbed over dubbing.

Dubbing—red D.F.M. wool.

Hackle—black hen.

Wings—barred teal, or grey squirrel or silver baboon.

Both the bodies of the Jersey Herd tube-fly and the Peter Ross may be dressed with bodies of silver or gold tinsel, as alternatives.

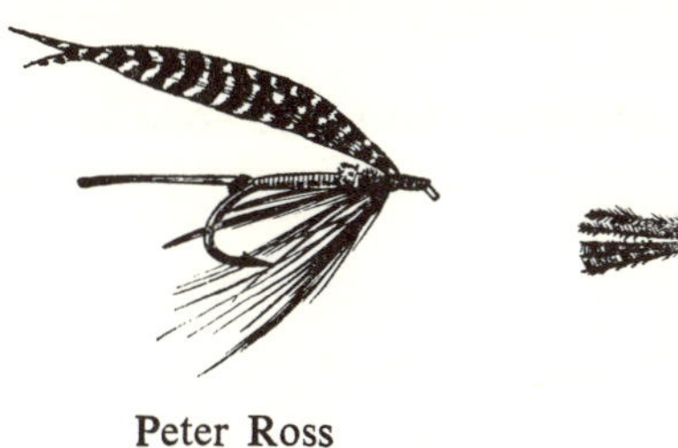

Peter Ross　　　　Jersey Herd

Black Lure

Alexandra　　　　Butcher

Buzzer Tactics

The Footballer (Chironomid pupa)

Footballer

Hook—14 to 16.
Body—alternate turns of black and white horsehair carried round the bend.
Thorax—mole's fur.
Head—peacock herl.

Black Buzzer

Hook—14 to 16.
Body—black floss silk rising to a hump for the thorax.
Ribbing—narrow silver lurex.
Head—peacock herl.

Green Buzzer

Hook—14 to 16.
Body—green fluorescent silk overwound with clear nylon or horsehair.
Thorax—green seal's fur.
Head—green ostrich herl.
The substitute of red materials makes the equivalent red buzzer.

Dry Buzzers

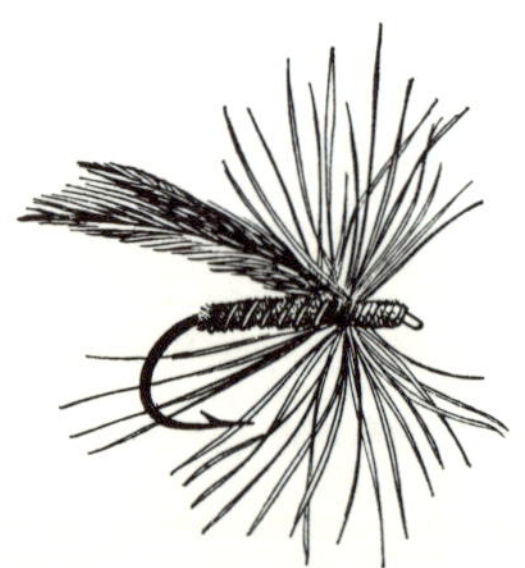

Dry Buzzer

To make the dry-fly equivalents of these pupae copies, it is only necessary to add a few turns of a matching cock's hackle. A pair of whitish hackle-point wings can be tied in to slope backwards along the hook shank for additional effect.

Brown Silverhorn

Hook—12

Body—dark green-olive tying silk.

Body hackle—dark brown cock, ribbed with gold wire.

Wings—waterhen (rolled).

Shoulder hackle—dark brown cock.

Horns—fibres of barred teal, tied in at the head to a length twice that of the body.

Cinnamon Sedge

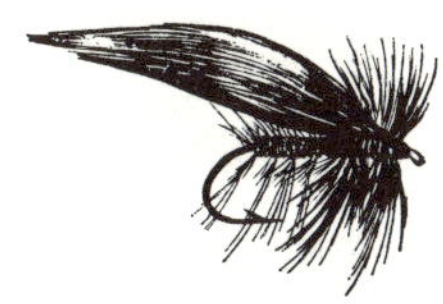

Cinnamon Sedge

Hook—12.

Body—fibres from the cinnamon tail feathers of a turkey.

Body hackle—ginger cock, ribbed gold wire.

Wings—landrail substitute (rolled).

Shoulder hackle—ginger cock.

Small Dark Sedge

Hook—14.

Body—maroon tying thread.

Body hackle—dark furnace, ribbed gold wire.

Wings—waterhen (rolled).

Shoulder hackle—dark furnace cock.

Great Red Sedge

Hook—6.

Body—mole's fur and claret seal's fur mixed together over a sliver of cork.

Body hackle—dark red cock, ribbed gold wire.

Wings—brown speckled hen (rolled).

Shoulder hackle—dark red cock.

Sedge Larvae

Hook—12 or 10 long shanked, wire loaded.
Tail—honey hen hackle points.
Body—cream floss silk, coated with cellulose varnish to which is stuck fragments of wood or grains of sand.
Head—peacock herl.

Invicta (Hatching Sedge)

Invicta

Hook—12 or 10.
Tail—golden pheasant crest.
Body—yellow seal's fur and D.F.M. wool mixed.
Body hackle—Red cock, ribbed gold lurex.
Wings—hen pheasant tail, tied low.
Shoulder hackles—red cock, and blue jay.

Cinnamon Sedge (Wet)

Hook—12 or 14.
Body—fawn floss silk.
Hackle—ginger hen.
Wings—brown hen, tied flat.

Ermine Moth

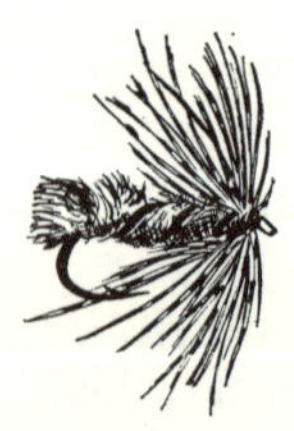

Ermine moth

Hook—12 to 8.
Tail—fluorescent orange wool.
Body—white rabbit ribbed with black wool.
Hackles—2 grey partridge.

Dayfly Tactics

Greenwell's Glory (Wet, for Olive nymphs)

Hook—12 or 14.
Body—primrose tying silk waxed with brown cobbler's wax, and ribbed gold wire.
Hackle—furnace hen.
Wings—starling.

Light Dayfly Dun (Wet)

Light Dayfly Dun (Wet)

Hook—12 or 14.
Body—greenish-yellow condor.
Hackle—furnace hen.
Wings—waterhen.

Dark Dayfly Dun (Wet)

Mallard & Claret

Greenwell's Glory (Wet)

Hook—12 or 14.
Body—dark brown condor.
Hackle—furnace hen.
Wings—grouse tail.

Hatching Dayfly (Gold-ribbed Hare's Ear)

Hook—12 or 14.
Body—hare's ear, ribbed narrow gold tinsel.
Legs and tail—fibres of the body-fur picked out with the dubbing needle.
Some fragments of teased-out D.F.M. wool can be worked in with the fur.

Mallard and Claret (Wet, for Sepia and Claret nymphs)

Hook—12 or 14.
Body—claret seal's fur mixed with mole, ribbed gold wire.
Wings—barred mallard.

Light Dayfly Dun (Dry)

Light Dayfly Dun (Dry)

Hook—14 to 12.
Body—greenish-yellow condor herl.
Hackle—light furnace cock.

Dark Dayfly Dun (Dry)

Dark Dayfly Dun (Dry)

Hook—14 to 12.
Body—dark brown condor herl.
Hackle—dark furnace cock.
Since bi-coloured hackles may be in short supply, light and dark red hackles may be substituted.

Dayfly Spinner (Dry)—Pheasant tail

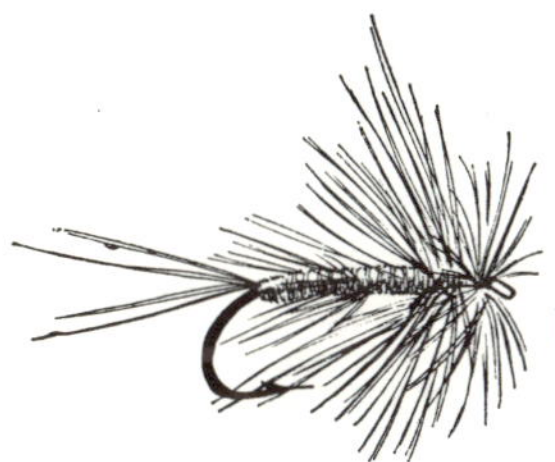

Pheasant tail

Hook—14 to 12.
Body—fibres from cock pheasant's tail, ribbed gold wire.
Hackle—light blue-dun cock.
To convert this to the "Spent Gnat", tie in two hackle points to lie flat at right angles to the hook-shank.

"Land-fly" Tactics

The Hoolet (*Large Brown Moth*)

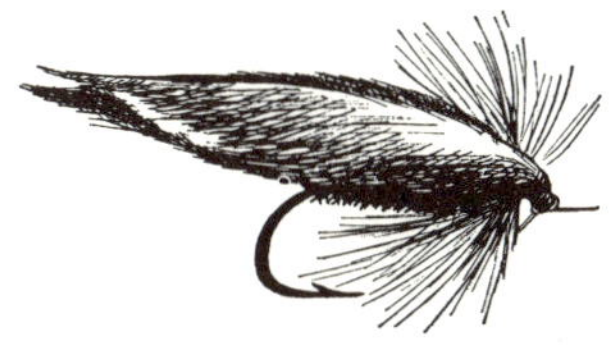

Hoolet

Hook—6.
Body—peacock herl over cork.
Hackle—brown cock (2).
Wings—brown owl (rolled).

Light Moth

Light moth

Hook—8 to 10.
Body—white fluorescent wool ribbed silver lurex.
Wings—white swan or brown owl, tied flat.

Crane Fly (*Daddy Longlegs*)

Crane fly

Hook—12.
Body—Detached plastic Mayfly body.
Legs—cock pheasant tail, knotted in the middle.
Wings—brown cock hackle points tied "spent".
Hackle—red cock.

Hawthorn Fly

Hawthorn fly

Hook—12.
Body—black ostrich herl.
Wings—pale starling, preferably tied forwards.
Hackle—black cock.

All the artificials in this section are dry-flies.

Tactics for sunk line

Corixa (point fly)

Hook—12, loaded with 5 amp fuse wire.
Body—white or cream floss silk or wool.
Ribbing—brown silk.
Wing cases—woodcock wing.
Legs—Buff hen, tied underneath and clipped short. The dropper fly is not wire-loaded, and the body has a cross-ribbing of silver lurex.

Caenis

The Grey Duster (Dry)

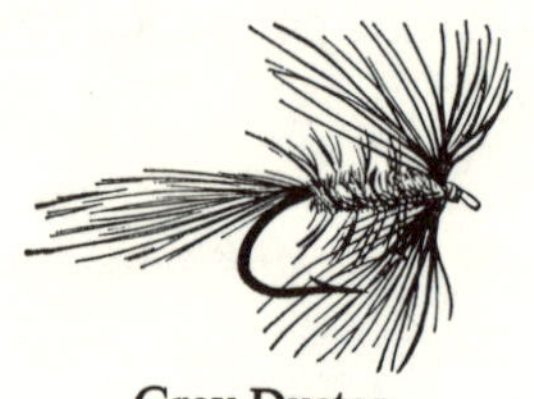

Grey Duster

Hook—16 to 18.
Tail—badger cock.
Body—rabbit spun onto brown silk tying thread.
Hackle—badger cock with well-marked "list".

Dragon-flies

Blue Damsel Nymph

Body—blue lurex ribbed with black wool on weighted tubes up to an inch long.
Hackle—blue guinea-fowl, or buck-tail.
Head—peacock herl.
A similar pattern is dressed using yellow-olive seal's fur for the body, and a gold-lurex ribbing, with matching hackle.

APPENDIX III

I HAVE found the following books to be of invaluable assistance in writing this book, and they are strongly recommended for further reading.

Fly Dresser's Guide, by John Veniard (A. & C. Black).
A Further Guide to Fly Dressing, by John Veniard (A. & C. Black).
A Dictionary of Trout Flies, by A. Courtney Williams (A. & C. Black).
An Angler's Entomology, by J. R. Harris (Collins).
Still Water Fly Fishing, by T. C. Ivens (Derek Verschoyle).
Lake Flies and their Imitation, by C. F. Walker (Herbert Jenkins).

INDEX